That Old Gang O' Mine

The Early and Essential
S.J. Perelman

I HAVE BRIGHT'S DISEASE
AND HE HAS MINE, SOBBED
THE PANTING PALOOKA

Pull in your beak, Durante, or some housewife'll be stealing it to stamp cookies with. "Does this parrot swear, my good man?" prattled a female poison in a pet-shop. "A little bit, mum," parried Mr. Pickerboom, "but he never shoots crap or goes out with chippies!" Just shot through and through with quiet wit, and you're probably hoping the same for the author.

That Old Gang O' Mine

The Early and Essential
S.J. Perelman

Edited by Richard Marschall

New York: William Morrow and Company, Inc., 1984

Introduction and Compilation copyright © 1984 by Richard Marschall

Most of the material in this book originally appeared in *Judge*, 1925–1931.

This book is dedicated to my father, Martin Marshall, Perelmaniac from the start; whose first purchase of *Judge* magazine was of the issue graced by this book's cover illustration; who believed all along.

Library of Congress Catalog Card Number: 84-60448

ISBN: 0-688-03199-4

Printed in the United States of America

First Edition

1 2 3 4 5 6 7 8 9 10

Art Director: Richard Marschall. Designer: Peppy White. Typesetting and Production: Kim Thompson, Steve Freitag, and Janet Toombs for Fantagraphic Books, Inc. The Introduction to this book originally appeared, in somewhat different form, in *NEMO: The Classic Comics Library*, 196 W. Haviland La., Stamford, CT 06903. Thanks, too, to Harriett Wasserman, agent extraordinaire, and to Harvey Ginsberg.

Contents

Introduction

Long before the *New Yorker* days, before his script work with the Marx Brothers, and earlier than even his most avid fans are aware, S.J. Perelman was an established American humorist, not only as a writer but as a popular cartoonist. This neglected period of Perelman's career is as rich in output as it is in quality, and *That Old Gang of Mine* marks both the first appearance of this work in book form and its first appearance in any form since original publication more than half a century ago (1925-1931).

Perelman fans will find that his style underwent a certain natural evolution, but the hallmarks of his writing—anarchic humor, unceasing wordplay, frenetic flights of free association transmitted in literate calmness—were present from the start. The sources of his inspiration were the reading matter he grew up with—the horsehair-sofa locutions of Victorian prose, the insipid glossiness of magazine advertising, the sappy, sentimental song lyrics of a generation previous to his, and the headlines from last week's tabloids. But his attitude and verbal gifts transmuted these banalities into a wit all his own.

The Twenties, the decade in which Perelman first appeared in print, was a remarkable period for American humor. ''College Humor'' was a field from which Perelman graduated in 1925, the year of his graduation from Brown University, where he had edited the campus humor magazine *Brown Jug*. At the time, every college of any size had its own thriving humor magazine, often with respectable sales to the general public; there were exchanges and reprints of the material in various journals; and a major national monthly, appropriately titled *College Humor*, thrived, largely on gatherings from these publications.

Among Perelman's generation were such rising stars as Robert Benchley, Robert E. Sherwood, and Gluyas Williams from the *Harvard Lampoon*; Theodor Geisel (Dr. Seuss) from the Dartmouth *Jack-o-Lantern*; Curtis Arnoux Peters (Peter Arno) from the Yale *Record*; Bennett Cerf and

Corey Ford from the Columbia *Jester*; and also at Brown were Quentin Reynolds and Perelman's future brother-in-law Nathaniel West. The Twenties provided fertile ground for an iconoclasm that these men both recorded and helped to define. They did not glorify the famed stereotypes of the Roaring Twenties—speakeasies, bathtub gin, rum-running, sheiks, and flappers—but rather utilized these subjects, antics, and "freedoms" of the postwar decade as objects of satire. That the writers often lived the lifestyles they lampooned did not affect their outlook; Perelman, for instance, was not alone among the writers who deplored Hollywood yet labored there. Everything in his field of vision was ridiculed, trivialized, exposed, and parodied and at the same time his sense of the absurd kept any sense of outrage in check.

Perelman's first major national "sale" was to *Judge* magazine, which each week highlighted gleanings from college humor publications. The magazine's motives may have been more mercenary than artistic—its budget was notoriously tight and such reprints were without fee. But through the early Twenties Perelman's cartoons were reprinted with increasing frequency, reaching an ever-larger number of readers.

The one reader who counted most was *Judge*'s own editor, Norman Anthony, who, if anyone is entitled to such a claim, could be called the discoverer of S.J. Perelman. Anthony himself was a mediocre cartoonist who found his metier first as Associate Editor of *Judge* in 1923 and then as full Editor the following year. (One of his first assistants, by the way, was Harold Ross, who presumably used his apprenticeship to learn what he thought a humor magazine should be. He rejected *Judge*'s tone, but it was not until the mid-1930s that he firmly overtook its popularity and circulation with *The New Yorker*.)

Anthony transformed the magazine into a raucous, irreverent, lively journal from the 40-year-old stodgy magazine it was. He sought out new artists and writers, crusaded against Prohibition, adopted a breezy design, and never hesitated to stoop to puns and slapstick. For more traditional fare he turned to George Jean Nathan and Pare Lorentz, theater and film critics, respectively.

One of the prize plums of Anthony's unceasing talent hunts, Perelman after graduation found himself a regular contributor of new material to *Judge* and was soon offered a contract to draw two cartoons and write one text piece a week.

The rediscovery of Perelman's cartoons should be a special delight to Perelman fans, for the drawings are filled with the allusions and metaphors with which his prose, then and later, constantly abounded. Many of the cartoons are the kind of illustrated cliches that throw light on his overall point of view; they are not mere sight gags.

In short order, he became one of the premier artists on the staff of the largest-circulation humor magazine in America. He once admitted that the

Voyageur—Ticket to Chefoo.
Agent—Change at Pekin.
Voyageur—No, damn it, I want my change now.

S.J. Perelman's first published cartoons were drawn for the humor magazine of Brown University, the *Brown Jug*. Perelman, a pre-med student, was editor of the magazine, his own contributions being almost exclusively cartoon work such as these three examples. From the start a prominent element of his humor was mockery of older and establishment-type humor (replaying the corniest of gags, taking ethnic jokes to the *n*th degree). Cartoonists on other college papers soon began to ape Perelman's approach and drawing styles, even after his graduation to the pages of *Judge*. Perelman was never, presumably, to think again of a doctor's career for himself.

"For vy you marry Abie's widow? She's old enough to be your mother vunce."
"I know, but Abie's clothes fit me like a glove."

Carpenter—That new wooden leg will cost you $10.
Sailor Fellow—What, are you going to charge me $10 for just remembering me?

great ambition of his boyhood was to be a cartoonist; he remembered drawing cartoons in his father's dry-goods store, using as paper the long cardboard strips around which bolts of fabric were wrapped.

His artwork had what may best be termed a bastard-woodcut look. Although most of the cartoons were pen-and-inks drawn to parody old woodcuts, many actually *were* block prints touched with pen and ink and Chinese white. Every drawing would parody either some moldy Victorian sentiment or some fusty scene from sources like Currier and Ives prints, *Godey's Lady's Book* or corny political broadsides. The legend beneath the drawing would be fully as dusty and cliched as the artwork, although often it would be totally irrelevant to the cartoon and, as the years passed, more laden with puns and Perelmanesque turns of phrase. Usually the caption would be a one-paragraph monologue never having any direct connection with the scene immediately to the north, and it would consist of a rickety chestnut of a joke, with slang and sarcasm grafted on.

Toward the end of the decade, as Perelman's prose pieces took on a more absurdist flavor, his cartoons became more abstract. He abandoned the woodcut style and drew in severe geometrical shapes. Soon there were no freehand lines at all, everything being drawn with templates and straight-edges. He repeated images within a drawing for no apparent purpose, and employed unpredictable shading devices. (One character's vest was patterned with a photographic detail of tenement windows—without the vaguest connection with the subject of the drawing or even its reliably unrelated caption.)

Perelman's graphics reflected his growing obsession with the trappings, and traps, of American culture. And by 1931 he evidently decided that the best way for him to deal with this subject matter was exclusively by the written word.

His signed articles in *Judge* had begun appearing regularly in the fall of 1926. His work betrays an admiration of George Ade's cynicism, Robert Benchley's nonsense and the observer's ear of Ring Lardner. He could be as insouciant as Stephen Leacock or as cantakerous as H.L. Mencken—sometimes in the same essay. Nor was he above self-mockery; Beau Perelman, Babs Perelman and Abu Ben-Perelman were personae he adopted.

Readers discovered him to be predictably unpredictable, a master of the absurd, an authority on patterns of speech and manners of writing—highbrow and lowbrow both—which he manhandled with ironic finesse. His written pieces soon took on categorization. One form was straight anecdotal narrative or a parody of contemporary pieces. Another was his own brand of stream-of-consciousness writing in which he kept the reader constantly off-guard with nonsequiturs, surreal turns of plot, and a veritable circus of verbal Rorschack-test inspirations.

All these devices, in early and late Perelman, can be grouped under the umbrella of Reductionism. He reduced literary pretension to meaningless-ness; he reduced the icons of our culture to absurdities. No play or book or song or social trend was safe when Perelman tiptoed up, disarmingly cradling his sledgehammer. He even reduced readers' comfortable expectations with every succeeding sentence. No wonder his pieces were never more than article-length—such roller-coaster rides in short trips were exhilarating; longer assaults on our assumptions would have been exhausting.

It doubtless was this assault style that attracted the Marx Brothers to Perelman. It was the material in *Judge*—not the *New Yorker* pieces of the mid-'30s or even the Broadway sketches he wrote in 1931 and '32—that brought Perelman to Hollywood in the Marx Brothers' employ. Even before the two men worked together, Groucho appeared in cartoons and text references, and he reciprocated by writing a blurb for Perelman's first book, *Dawn Ginsbergh's Revenge:* "From the moment I picked up your book until I put it down, I was convulsed with laughter. Some day I intend reading it."

Given their shared predilections and poses, collaboration between the Marx Brothers and Perelman seems to have been inevitable. Perelman has recorded the grueling association of doing screenplays for the Brothers in Hollywood, the trauma of that town's lifestyle, the boorishness of the movie community; but one suspects a bit of literary, if not historical, license in his reminiscences of those days. He did, after all, work on *two* movies for the Marx Brothers, *Monkey Business* and *Horse Feathers*, as well as nine other screenplays. The personalities of S.J. Perelman and the Marx Brothers may not have been attuned, but their styles—anarchic humor loosely garbed in playful irreverence—were.

Perelman once told me that he considered that his career began when he sold his first piece to *The New Yorker* (1934). Perhaps this feeling can be traced to the real conflicts that did accompany his association with the Marx Brothers and to the fact that during his *Judge* days he thought of himself primarily as a cartoonist, not an essayist.

Even so, there is no mistaking Perelman's unique genius in these articles. His frequent reference to contemporary events and personalities may escape some readers today, but a concordance for his props is hardly necessary. One striking difference between these early articles and the later Perelman is a real sense of spontaneity that perhaps inevitably declined through the years. Also one gets the sense that the sardonic face of Perelman, when assumed, is more feigned here than in later writings.

Perelman also told me that I had a larger collection of these old articles and cartoons than he did. Whatever the reason—Hollywood, Broadway, his declining interest in drawing cartoons, *Judge's* eventual insolvency—Perelman himself never put any of these essays and drawings in book form. And eventually the scarcity of old copies of *Judge*, which it has taken several decades to collect, has, until now, kept from us this early and essential S.J. Perelman.

—Richard Marschall
Billingsgate
Weston, Conn.

That Old Gang O' Mine

The Early and Essential
S.J. Perelman

Puss in Boots

This story starts off about a miller, so we better pull the old gag: Why does a miller wear a white hat? Answer, to cover his head! Ha! ha! We fooled you! Well, anyway, once upon a time there was a miller who was so poor when he died that all he left his three sons was a mortgage, a piece of pork, and a cat. The two oldest sons drew the mortgage and the pork, so they went into the real estate and meat business and made good. But the third son who got the cat was sore and contested the will, but the lawyers got everything and he had to fall back on the cat. Well, one day he was sitting in a subway station and he says to the cat, "Well, Morris, after I eat you and sell your skin, what will I do then? I ask you." The cat thinks a while and says, "Be your age, Irving (that was the name). All I want is a burlap bag and a pair of boots and I will get you out of this jam." "Ha!" says Irving, "are you trying to be English, calling shoes boots?" But he gave the cat the bag and the boots and away he went.

Marquis Irving falls into the drink.

He hung around a cornfield for a while and argued with a couple of rabbits till they walked into the bag; then he took them to the king of that country and says, "Here is a present from my boss, Marquis Irving." The king was overcome with joy, as he and his beautiful daughter Sybil had been living on pretzels and port wine for years. The next day the cat showed up with half a dozen spring chickens and told the same story. He did this for a week, each time bringing some choice goody. Then one day he read in the paper where the king was going to take a spin in his new model Ford with Sybil. So he went to Irving and told him to make believe he was drowning in a river that the king was going to pass. Irving didn't want to do it at first because his life insurance had just ran out, but the cat threatened him and finally he gave in.

So when the king drove by the river he heard a yell for help and all of a sudden the cat dives out of the bushes and says that his boss, Marquis Irving, has fell into the drink and will the king save him. The king threw Irving a life preserver he had in the back of the car and then the cat pulled a hard luck fable about robbers running off with Irving's suit while he was in swimming. So the king gave Irving a swell new pair of flannel pants with only a little hole in them and a tweed coat which was too small for anybody in the palace and Irving looked simply perfect. The king invited Irving to take a drive with him and Sybil and all through it Sybil kept her eyes on him like he was the lucky number in a lottery. Suddenly they came to a field and the king says, "What a swell field! Who owns it?" And a workman which had been tipped off by the cat pipes up and says, "Marquis Irving, none other." So the king began to think of Irving as a son-in-law already.

In the meantime the cat had run ahead and come to the apartment of an ogre named Bernstein. An ogre is something that looks like all the parts Lon

Chaney ever played rolled together. The cat walks in on the ogre and says, "Good afternoon, Mr. Bernstein. I understand you can change yourself into anything you want to." "Yeh," says Bernstein and with that he turns into a vacuum cleaner and chases the cat up the side of the wall. "Ha! ha!" says the cat, "That sure was a laugh on me. Now I don't like to seem catty, but I bet you can't change into a mouse." Bernstein immediately turns into a mouse and the cat jumps on him and wipes the floor with him.

A minute later the king and Sybil and Irving pulled up at the door. "What a swell apartment!" says the king. "Who owns that?" And the cat, which was smoking a cigar on the steps says, "It belongs to Marquis Irving, no kidding!" Then the king turns to Irving. "Young man," he says, "you've got a great fortune. How would you like to marry a princess?" So Irving takes the hint and marries Sybil and the old man took him into the firm and gave him the New England territory with a straight salary and commission. So they moved to Long Island with the twelve sets of oyster forks they got for presents. The cat is now president of a large corporation which proves that any boy can make good.

The Sleeping Beauty

Prince Dave and the Sleeping Beauty.

Now here is a swell yarn we found at the bottom of a box of iron fillings and we said right away, we owe it to our dear public to show it to them. Once upon a time there was a king and queen named Morton Steinberg and his wife Fannie. Morton and Fannie had everything they wanted, even an electric fan in the hot weather. They were both kind and wise and their subjects were fairly daffy over them. But there was one thing they lacked: the patter of baby feet. They made up their minds that if they ever had a child they would name it Shirley, even if it was a boy. Well, one day the king came home and found the little wife tatting a pair of bootees, so he tiptoes over to her and then there was a slow fade-out with blurred sub-titles and an art decoration of a stork carrying a baby.

Well, they threw a real party for Shirley's christening. They had a cornet band from the Bronx and the caterer was paid strictly in advance. The king and queen invited seven good fairies named Brodsky as godmothers, and the good wishes they piled on Shirley, you never heard anything like it. But Morton and Fannie had forgot to send a ticket to an old fairy named Lulu Belle, which lived around the corner and the old lady was peeved. But she came anyway and right in the middle of all the predictions of good luck, she pipes up and says, "When that kid grows up she will cut her hand on a gin bottle and die of exposure!" So then there was a riot and everybody yelled, "Throw her out, Levine!" (Levine was the caterer.) But all of a sudden

another fairy raps for silence and says, "I got another wish left! The kid won't die, but will go to sleep for a hundred years. And then a handsome prince will get her out of the coma and she will marry him!" And right after that there was a loud noise like an airplane and all the fairies left for a convention in Atlantic City.

Well, King Morton and Queen Fannie were determined not to let the princess pop off into a trance, so they posted a notice saying that from then on, nobody would be allowed to drink gin. This was called Prohibition and it was very successful (remember, this is a fairy tale). But one day when Morton was on the road and Mrs. Steinberg was playing bridge, little Shirley, which by this time had grown up to be another Gloria Swanson in looks, happened to amble up to an attic in the palace. And there was an old lady pouring herself a hooker of Gordon water. So Shirley said, "I beg your pardon, but what is

that?" "Oh, hello!" said the old dame. "You wouldn't remember what that is, but I'll tell you: it's shoe polish!" So they both winked at each other and the old timer handed Shirley the bottle and the latter tossed off a drink that would have staggered General Grant. But by accident she dropped the bottle and a piece of the glass cut her finger. And the next minute she was snoring away in a corner. And the funny part of all this was that the whole castle fell asleep with her.

Well, about a hundred years later a nifty prince named Dave Rifkowitz was in charge of that territory and he was overtaken by a storm one night, so he stopped at a farmer's house and the farmer said he could stay there, but there was only one bed—oh, pardon us! That's another story... Well, anyway, a prince came to this castle and rang the bell but the maid must have taken the day off or something. So he went in and found everybody asleep, even the telephone operator, but he wasn't surprised at that. Then all of sudden he came to the princess's room and there she was snoozing on the bed. She looked even prettier than when she fell asleep, because she had had her face lifted in the meanwhile. So he woke her up and showed her his credentials and she said she was crazy about him already and did he have the ring

IS IT HOT ENOUGH FOR YOU?

All ladies and children under fourteen should not listen to the following: Sadie, who suffers from the heat, could bear it no longer and remarked to her friend, Sir Henry: "Gee whiz, Johnny, wouldn't it be swell if a plate of ice cream should come right up out of the floor in front of me?" Sir Henry, who is a "joshing" fellow, retorted instantly. "Oh, no, I'd hate to have a coolness spring up between us!" This novel aspect of the situation took the big cash prize.

with him. And after he said yes, she told him to wake up all the people in the castle while she ran around the corner and had her hair waved. And then they got married and had twelve children, all girls and one homelier than the other. The lesson here is that one should leave sleeping dogs lie.

The Frog Prince

The frog turns into a handsome young sheik.

Once upon a time there was a king who had three daughters and every one of them a wow. But times was hard so one of them went in the chorus, while another got a good job in a five-and-dime store as a cash girl. But the third one, a creature named Dora, was too lazy even to lift her feet out of the oven if her shoes were burning. Well, one day Dora was lying out in the garden shaking out sevens with a pair of dice when one of the bones rolled into a nearby pond. Dora tried to fish it out with a hairpin, but for once this handy article was no use, and just as Dora was seeing rosy pictures of her old man, the king, giving her a clip on the ear, a voice from the pond says:

"Say, kid, would you like to get back that there dice?"

For a minute Dora thought it was one of them Channel swimmers or something; then she collected her wits, which wasn't much, and replies:

"Say, would I like a swell corned-beef sandwich with mustard and a stein of steam beer? You bet I want that dice!"

And with that a frog hops out of the pond and says, "Well, I ain't got no corned-beef sandwich with steam beer, but I can get you that dice. But you got to promise to let me sit near you when you eat and also to let me drink out of your cup and sleep under your bed."

"Is there anything else?" says the girl sarcastically, but she thought, why not promise this dopey frog and then I can always laugh it off. So she tells him to go ahead and the sky's the limit, if he only gets the dice back.

A second later the frog hops out of the drink and hands her the dice. "How about that agreement?" he asks.

"What agreement?" says the gold digger. "I never signed no contract!" And then she turns on her heel and leaves the frog crestfallen.

Well, just as the king and his daughters were sitting down to supper in the kitchen, there's a rap on the door and a voice outside says, "Dora, open the door!" So Dora goes to the door and who should it be but the frog. He leaps in and goes over to the king and tells him the whole story, how Dora had two-timed him and he would see his lawyer. The old man got scared and ordered his daughter to go through with the agreement. Then the frog made Dora feed him with her own spoon and she nearly got the heebies doing it. After dinner the old man and the frog smoked a good cigar and talked and then the frog turns to Dora.

"Well, kid," he says, "now I've got to sleep; I've got an important conference to-morrow."

So the frog follows her upstairs and when she got up there she was so mad she grabbed him and threw him against the wall with enough force to get her a job with the Giants. And with that the frog turns into a perfect sheik with shiny black hair and a small roadster, who said he had been turned into a frog by an old widow in the next block who was jealous of him. Dora fell in love with him right away and when the old man saw him he gave the couple his blessing and the price of a license and they got married as soon as the former frog had got a raise in the delicatessen store where he was working. This story shows what hard luck is it to shoot crap.

Homer Veppy or How One Boy Found Himself

Homer Veppy was not like other boys. From the first he was fascinated by books. When other lads of his age were hallooing at their cricket, Homer could generally be found somewhere about the piggery—or, as it was then called, the hoggery—busy with his book. At first he found a simple pleasure in taking the pages out one by one and burying them; later, he learned how to build swell bonfires, which, in his own childish way, he called potato bakes. Only, instead of using potatoes, he used books. In this way he went through an entire set of Balzac, most of Kipling, and a good portion of Rabelais. He was also fond of the modern authors.

It was quite early in his life that his peculiarities began to appear. When he was twelve years old, his father woke up one day—or rather didn't wake up—to find that his precocious lad had smothered him while he slept. His mother, of course, had remonstrated with the growing boy. He promised to be good, and for a time all went well. Then, one day, judge of his mother's surprise to find on her return home that Homer had barbecued his older sister Frugalia, aged fourteen. There was Frugalia frying on a spit, astonishment writ large all over her face, while Homer busied himself with his blocks on the floor.

"Now, Homer," began Mrs. Veppy, "this will never do—"

"But, Mother," explained the smooth-faced prodigy, "she smokes so nicely!" In the face of this what could a mother do? She could only take Homer on her lap and explain that nice girls never smoked, and

"At twenty-five Homer was ready for college..."

that in the future such things would be forbidden. With tears in his eyes, Homer promised.

Time passed, and Homer grew older. His twenty-fifth year found him ready for that greatest of adventures—college.

There was a touching scene on the eve of his leave taking. At his mother's knee stood Homer idly dissecting the cat with a fork. His mother, her eyes suspiciously bright, handed him a Colt .44 and his father's razor.

"Homer, bairn," said Mrs. Veppy softly, "what do you want to be when you grow up?"

"I don't know, mammy," replied Homer, "but I often felt I'd like to be a street car conductor."

"Then you shall go to Harvard," said Mrs. Veppy, or rather Mrs. Fitznagle, for by this time she had married again, which really made Homer a Fitznagle, didn't it?

The first five years of Homer's college life passed smoothly enough. He joined an exclusive eating club and kept on with his books. In his second year the club moved on to a new house, as there had been a fire in the old one in which five of the brothers had been roasted to a turn. I daresay the boys would have been piqued had they known that Homer lit the fire, but he never squealed on a pal. At the end of his third year an uneventful incident nearly ended Homer's college career. He was discovered slicing the dean into small

Said one lad to another: "The guy who lives next door to me is building a hill in his back yard," and the other lad retorted: "What, Oxtail, are you letting him put up a bluff like that?" He was quite a wag.

THERE IS NOT NO SANTY CLAUS BARKED THE YOUNG AGNOSTIC

Well, men, here's to the confusion of Cromwell and the happy restoration of Charles the Second! That reminds me of the one they're passing around in Paris just now. "Bridget, for dinner we'll have boiled mutton with caper sauce," directed Mrs. Patterson. "Please, sor, there's a divil a bit of capers we have in the house at present," countered Bridget. "Then go out in the garden and cut some!" authorized the pretty lady as she stepped aboard the boat train for Cherbourg.

LOOK INTO MY EYES CLARA AND TELL ME YOU STILL CARE

They tell me Dempsey's going to fight Paul Whiteman in Chicago in the fall, but you can't fool me; Whiteman is a poet, not a boxer. Look this one over, customers: A teacher asked one of the dummies, "What became of Sodom and Gomorrah?" "They were destroyed," replied Hal Roach. "And what became of Tyre?" she asked. "It was punctured, heh heh heh heh heh!" declared the little wretch. They ought to boil those little wisecrackers in Crisco.

segments; the affair was hushed up with difficulty, but the dean was very formal with Homer for a time.

But they soon surprised everyone by strolling arm in arm across the yard, the best of chums; for Homer, in his own unconscious way, had done the dean a great favor. He had been lounging in his window absently dropping flower-pots filled with gravel on the heads of passers-by when he scored a bull's-eye in the form of the president himself, whose chagrin was laughable indeed. Shortly afterward the dean became president and a fast friend of Homer's.

The next two years, however, wrought an immense change in the boy. It was after a separation of a year that his mother noticed a new Homer. She finally took him aside and looked into his eyes.

"Homer," she asked, "what is this change that has come over you?"

"Mamma," said Homer slowly, "I don't want to be no street car conductor."

"What!" cried the poor woman, "what have I sent you to Harvard for—" But the boy interrupted her. From his brief case he had taken a magazine.

"I see my mistake," he said. "What I really wanted to be was a motorman. And here is the magazine that helped me find myself." And he handed her a copy of *Vanity Fair*.

Brave Deeds of Bright Boys

How Archie McOsker Saved a Man's Life

Archie McOsker was twelve years old and and in his second year in primary school. One day Archie was just about to leave a barroom when he saw near him an old man who had arranged seven glasses of Antigua rum in front of him and was preparing to down them one after the other. The old man was pretty well shot already, and Archie, taking in the situation in a glance, realized that seven more would probably prove fatal. With a bound he was at the side of the old man and before the latter could speak, Archie had tossed them off himself without batting an eyelash. The old man turned out to be none other than Goody Two Shoes and he rewarded the daring lad liberally for his brave action. Archie finished his schooling the following year with the old man's assistance and is now a rising cash boy in a meat market.

Tommy and His Fish

Tommy in only four years old but he is already very fond of "the finny sport." Tommy's collection of fish, which he keeps under his bed, includes one squid, a score of eels, a lovely little trout as good as new, and a perfet honey of a slightly used ham sandwich. Tommy never tires, however, of telling how he hooked his biggest fish. Let us hear him tell it himself:

"It was at a night club," says Tommy, "and we had gone about half the evening when I found out that I had left my billfold in my other pants, heh, heh... Just then I saw this waiter approaching with the check. I turned to the other gent in the party, a citrus man from the West, and told him I had to make a call. Then I ducked around the corner and in two minutes I was out on the main drag heading for my crib. Say, that was a close call!"

Tommy and his fish.

The Kiddies' Own High Hat Junior

Well, well, and how are all the little demi-wits to-day? Heard a good one yesterday. . . . seems they are calling camels "Ships of the Desert" because they carry so much baggage across the desert. . . . ha, ha. . . . . Speaking of camels, they may be able to go a whole week without a drink, but *we'd* get thirsty!. . . . . Little Henry Firefogel, of New Rochelle, sends in this interesting recipe: "Two parts of buttermilk, one part of water, and a spoonful of sugar. Shake well with shaved ice and heave it out the window. It's no damn good anyway." Thanks, Henny. . . . . we'll try it. . . . . Read a good book the other day. . . . it was called "How Elsie Found Herself". . . . and tells how Elsie found herself a platinum bracelet, a new Royce, and a sugar poppa. . . . . Everybody around here seems to be playing this new game, "Anecdotes". . . . you start off with the one about the pair that were traveling and the hotel that was filled up and so on; then the person next to you tells one and so on. . . . then gradually all the decent people leave the room and the last person in the room is made into a salad. . . .'At's hot!

The six best "Junior Steppers":

"Waltz Me Around Again, Willie."

"I Found a Rose in the Devil's Garden."

"Suite 31, for Piccolo and Chin Rest" (Brahms).

"The Merry King of England."

"How Toby Got Fried" (Recitation).

"Jerusalem the Golden."

A Playtime Song

Ring-a-ring-o'-roses,
    That's the game to play.
In the shady orchard
    On a summer's day;
While the birds above us,
    In the apple tree,

Peep at us and wonder
   What our game can be.

   Chorus

Red hot mamma,
Red hot mamma,
Turn your dampers down!
Ring-a-ring-o'-roses,
   Baby's tumbled down,
Pick her up, the darling—
   Kiss away the frown!
Tumbles never hurt one
   Where the grass is green.
Put her in the middle,
   Baby shall be queen!

   OSCAR WILDE at the age of ten
Oscar Wilde, boy marvel, who swam from Yonkers to
Buffalo in two hours recently. Oscar says laughingly
that he has just washed his hair and can't do a thing
with it.

The Handy Girl Around the House: How to Make a Sugar Papa

Any girl who is clever with her hands or feet can easily make a sugar papa.
This handy article around the house can always be used for a variety of
purposes and a good deal of innocent fun as well as profit can be had from
him. There are two kinds of sugar papas (1) Big wash-tub manufacturers, and
(2) Big millinery men. These two classes are just in from Fort Wayne, where
they are big shots but too well-known to shake a loose ankle with the gals.
Consequently they propose to dye the hamlet a rich magenta by next Friday
night before rolling into the Buffalo sleeper.

   The best place to start making a sugar papa is at ringside in any good night-
club about twelve-thirty. The general procedure is as follows: The girl should
gaze around the tables, taking careful note of the more eligible papas. A safe
rule to follow in selecting one's quarry is, the fatter the papa, the fatter the

bankroll. After our girl has satisfied herself that she sees her proper choice, she should give him the dazzling orbs for several moments, and then look away quickly. A moment later she may look back and then break into the full thirty-two-tooth spread of welcome. In five minutes the papa will be planted at her table trying to force down another cocktail. In ten minutes papa will be retailing the wise one about the taxidermist which he got off at the Lions clam-bake last summer, and in fifteen minutes he will be making a date for tomorrow afternoon in front of Cartier's.

More important than making a sugar papa is keeping him clean once you have made him. There are several good methods. If the day is cold, our girl may allow her teeth to chatter and then very casually pull the one about the semi-annual fur sales they are having. A little baby talk may be used, and a judicious kiss on the bald spot now and then. One's oldest hosiery should be worn when meeting papa for the second time, and when he notices all the runs, a little catch in the voice and a couple of Grade A tears will usually bring around a dozen pairs of serviceable stockings.

Whenever Papa gets dirty, he should be cleaned thoroughly at once. With good care one may train a papa to become very devoted and faithful; after a time he will speak only when spoken to and will follow you around with his fountain pen in his hand ready to dash off the checks.

There are all sorts of games one may play with her papa, depending on his disposition. If it is a gray day and papa's spirits are low, one of the best games is "Shake-Down." This is played as follows: One girl pulls the racket about needing a new pair of shoes and my word, how do you expect a girl to walk up Madison

WHEN THE CATS AWAY THE MICE WILL PLAY

Said a New York belle to her country cousin, not having seen her for a long while, "Come, let us have a little drink after our long separation."

"Oh, yes, indeed," replied the ingenuous farmer's daughter. "For, when we do see each other, it's meet and drink."

And both laughed, heartily.

Avenue in her stocking feet. Papa growls and says he's been shelling out too long and he's tired of being the fall guy. Then our girl smiles sweetly and says maybe if she wrote a letter to somebody's wife out in Fort Wayne...Beige lizard kicks are being worn a good deal this season, although gray and black sharkskin with mottled green inserts is considered chic.

Another hot pastime is "Reproaches." This is also a game for papa's low days; he will generally begin with the wild surmise that our girl cares only for his money. This is the signal for her to throw her arms around daddy and start reproaching. "Why, Elmer, you little funny, you know I'd care *just* as much for you if you didn't have a dime!" And then, a moment later, "But you really *have* some left, haven't you, darling?" This is a strong, serviceable line and bears repetition. A few sniffs and the good old Damp Handkerchief Dabbing at the Eyes goes big.

And finally, a little note on letters. Your duty to yourself, the tabloids, and the District Attorney demands that you guard papa's letters very carefully. For who knows when papa's devotion will cool and there will be no more benzine in your cigarette lighter? Even if you never use the letters, they make rich reading to the next one.

Forging Ahead in Business

By S. J. Perelman (A Lad with VISION)

I will tell you a STORY. It is a SHORT story. But it has a POINT. And if you are AGGRESSIVE and DISSATISFIED with your $20 a week job as a SHIPPING CLERK, you will LEARN something.

The other day I was passing by a PRIMARY SCHOOL at recess time. On the sidewalk was a TOT playing twenty-one or fantan or something with his MARBLES. I stooped down and TOOK AWAY his marbles from him. He stood up, TEARS streaming from his childish eyes, and he said, "Mister, don't TAKE AWAY them there marbles of mine!" I CONFRONTED him. I said, "If you were a MAN," I said, "you wouldn't CARE. You would go out and GET AGATES!" The LITTLE FELLOW squared his shoulders and THRUST OUT his jaw. "I will!" he said through clenched teeth. "I'm going out and get AGATES!" "Go ahead," I said, "and I hope you get two black eyes and CHICKEN-POX while you're out there!" And I turned on my HEEL.

Gentlemen, today that little TOT is GROVER CLEVELAND. And why NOT? Anybody who is sick of MARBLES can easily go out and get AGATES. If you are DISGRUNTLED, SORE, FULL OF AMBITIONS, DESIRES, INHIBITIONS, or GREEN STRIPE, you TOO can change NOW. How can you FORGE AHEAD?

Let me answer that by ANOTHER story. During the Spanish WAR, a company of ZOUAVES was trapped in a gully named Ginsberg by a troop of Spaniards. Fearing that reinforcements would arrive too late, Peckinpaugh, who commmanded the Zouaves, slipped a note in a bottle and threw it OVERBOARD. The intrepid band was captured shortly after by the fierce Mexican GUERILLAS and had to eat SAWDUST. Realizing that SCURVY would result if his men had to GO ON eating sawdust, Peckinpaugh swam to Morro Castle and returned with a live CHICKEN in his teeth. This ACT of HEROISM saved the DAY and later resulted in Peckinpaugh being awarded the FIRST PRIZE of twenty-five dollars. His essay was entitled "How My Dog Shep Trapped the Old Woodchuck."

Fellows, if Peckinpaugh and Grover Cleveland could do what they did, you CERTAINLY could. So REMEMBER: FRIDAY night in the VESTRY and every little MAN JACK of you bring his UNIFORM and HATCHET. RAY HIGGINBOTHAM will lead the older boys and Francis Snodgrass the younger ones. And after the HIKE, oh, boy! All the HOT DOGS you can eat and PLENTY of cider! Don't forget—eight o'clock, Friday night, rain or moonshine and FREE ADMISSION. LET'S GO!!

That Old Gang O' Mine

Well, well, how time does fly! This morning I was looking through my memory-book, and, girls, it sure drew the old tears to my eyes! All those old friends, all the jolly times, all gone, all gone! There was one picture in particular which carried me back. It's this "snap" I took of the "bunch" in good old Public School 93, Borough of Queens. There they are, my five inseparable pals, cheery laughing good fellows all. Look at them: good nature, comradeship, clean fun bubbling out of every —— face in the lot.

The two fellows on the left are the two Pickerbaugh brothers, whom the world knows as the two Pickerbaugh brothers. Staunch friends, a bit serious but always ready for a prank or innocent lark. They're out in St. Helena now,

ANHEUSER BUSCH

THIS WILL REVOLUTIONIZE SCIENCE PREDICTED BUSCH

"Mama!" begged Toby Riskin of that person, "may I go over to Gedney Hirschbaum's house?" "Is that the boy who has the charades all the time?" inquired staunch Mrs. Riskin. "Yeh," spake Toby. "No, you can't," denied the fond parent. "You should go playing with a boy with infectious diseases like that? Act your age!" Toby was so incensed that he laid her out cold with a hay-maker to her chin.

JUST THREE JOLLY GOOD FELLOWS ON A BENDER(?)

Would you like to hear one about two elevator boys? Well, probably not, but you're going to hear it anyway. Said one of them, "By the way, Giles, a gent offered to bet me one thousand smackers against my five hundred that Jess Willard would knock out Jack Johnson!" "And what did you do?" queried Giles, shifting the quid to his other cheek. "Oh, I took him up at once!" sallied Jerry Kornbloom, not without humor, we think. Well, so long, I'll see you in the funny papers!

doing well in the grocery business, bless their souls! And next to them Harry Lefkowitz, who is none other than good old "Jimmie" Walker, our Mayor. Harry was the wit of the "bunch" and always had a laughing retort or ready quip on his tongue's end. I remember the time he said to a teacher, "Say, you remind me of a pie!" "How's that?" asked Mr. McCracken, the physics teacher. "Because you got such a crust!" smiled Harry, and the laughter was universal. Great boy, Harry. Too bad he died.

And then, next to him, old "Peaches" Faunce. What a comrade he was! He was great on imitations; you should have heard him. He could imitate anything, but his specialty was imitating an old sow in the barnyard who'd found out that her bank balance was overdrawn. He used to have us in a stitch. I heard recently that he went in the insurance game up in Providence R.I., and if good nature and warm friendship mean anything, "Peaches" will go far in the lumber business. Good luck, Fauncey, old kid!

And "last but not least," there was good old John McGraw. There was a good story about John; he'd been kicked in the head by a horse and they had to put a silver plate in his head. We used to "kid" him a lot, as the saying goes, and Quent Pickerbaugh said, "I wish I was as lucky as you, being born with a silver plate in your head!" Old Quent was a card, sure enough!

Well, so it goes! Here today and gone tomorrow! That's life. But I always say, there's nothing like getting out the old pictures and looking through them and then tying them up in a good fat bundle and heaving them in the ash-can. I guess I'm sentimental, but after all, old faces are the best, and gosh, how I'd love to see that old gang o' mine!

How to Board a Street-Car

A good deal has been said and written lately about the proper way to board a street-car. Anyone who would be swagger or chic must know that there is only one way—the right way—to board this newest of all fads, as it has been termed. Hence, a few timely suggestions.

The ordinary street-car, as a rule, is not a heavy feeder, but his diet must be varied if you would have him free from scurvy. A few fresh vegetables served with the meat course will keep your pet in trim. I would advise cutting out starchy foods altogether, as starch eventually turns to sugar and forms a coating over the street-car, which is illy suited to that "monarch among animals," to apply a popular name. Who has not seen some poor street-car ambling aimlessly along, thickly coated with sugar? Is there a sadder sight? Answer: No. Plain, wholesome foods and thick, nutritious soups like beef-broth, barley and boiled onions will make the ideal diet for an anaemic street-car, and a little fresh gruel thinned with warm milk will work wonders for him when he is indisposed. Do not wait for cavities to appear. Be sure that your toothbrush is not too large for your mouth; many a man has been inadvertently cut off in his prime by swallowing a toothbrush.

And, above all, keep away from your lodge if your feet trouble you. Many a serious case of club feet could have been avoided if the feet's owner had only sat at home instead of gone traipsing around to visit the boys. A stitch in time saves nine, says the old saw, and God help you if they have to stitch your feet. It's bad enough when they stitch your shoes, let alone your feet. Think it over, boys, and when you come across some more of that tin-foil, don't throw it away. Think of our boys in the trenches without toothbrushes and do your bit toward crushing the dread Hun menace. You can go now, children, but I'd like to see Titheradge, Todhunter, Apthorpe, Aspinwall, Rapfogel, and Flowers for a minute.

Dance Madness in Coney Island

By Beau Perelman

The "grizzly bear" is quite the thing in

CONEY ISLAND

and "lordy how you can hug"

Coney Island, July 15—Everybody who is anybody at all (and most everybody is somebody) at this fashionable watering-place has gone made over the latest big flash in dancing, the "Grizzly Hug." Nightly the casinos and *cafes chantants* are crowded with members of the smart world absorbed in learning the step, and wherever one goes he hears the new "ragtime" piece, "Valencia," which is closely associated with this dance. At the "Idyllic Houre" and the "Dew Droppe Inne," the two best-known dancing places, Syncopating Sammy Sheffers and his Six Sardonic Saxophonists weave orgies of orchestration as the intent devotees of Terpsichore trip the light fantastic toe. Here one sees hundred-year-old dowagers dancing with young scions of noble houses and youthful "flappers" threading the intricate maze with bored clubmen and raconteurs.

The dance was introduced into this exclusive summer colony by Phil and Maizie Lukin, late of the Club Makowitz, Piccadilly; the pair are shown dancing in the magnificent ballroom of the Fishbein Arms before an audience which numbers among those present such distinguished guests as Bishop Irving Shapiro of the Bronx and "Lucky Frankie" Hanley, the Flying Fenian, who made the first non-stop record between four speakeasies. The Light-footed Lukins, as they are billed, run an estaminet and hot-dog kennel on the Boardwalk during the day and in the evening give lessons to those who would be *au courant*.

Almost as "catchy" a tune as "Valencia" is the enormously popular "I Wanna Wander Back to Bay Ridge, Brooklyn," the work of the prolific young composer, Johnny Bach, who plays here this season at the Orliansky Roof with his orchestra, "Johnny Bach's Boyish Bummers." The Orliansky Roof is perhaps the most correct place to dine and dance, as no rubber sneakers are allowed and shirts are compulsory.

Men who know Coney Island say that there is a possibility of its becoming a rather well-known resort if the dance furor continues, although the exclusive residents seem loath to encourage newcomers outside their set. There have been rumors that amusements such as roller-coasters, ferris-wheels, and side-shows will be introduced shortly, but small credence can be attached to them. Coney Island, we predict, will always rank as the playground of the "upper crust."

A FLIGHTY PAIR

"Don't breathe a word, Casper—but I think Lord Percy is horribly fastidious."
"You said it, Dalmatia. He even insists upon being measured for his coat-of-arms."

The Black Buzzard of Britain

He battled with death in the skies—for an idea—and won, but the price he paid—

The story of the great English ace, Major S.J. (Peaches) Perelman, as told to himself by S.J. Perelman.

Ten thousand feet above the barren waste of No Man's Land, on the afternoon of June 23, 1915, there took place one of the most thrilling encounters that the secret archives of any European country boast. Tense at the controls of his giant Walkover Narrow-Vamp bombing plane, Major Sir Sidney Derek Jeremy Perelman, known to the brother officers of his regiment as Peaches, narrowed his eyes to mere pin-points of light as the huge bird of prey climbed higher and higher into the rarefied atmosphere. Seven thousand five hundred feet below small puffs of smoke were all that marked the presence of embattled Europe. Behind the daring Major in the cockpit sat "Nervous George" O'Shaughnessy of the Royal Flying Corps, and grim-jawed Death rode on the fuselage (not bad, hey, boys?).

They had reached an altitude of over nine thousand feet when the indomitable pilot turned from his controls to O'Shaughnessy.

"George," he said, "George, are we alone?"

"Practically," replied George, fumbling in his vest pocket; "that is, except for grim-jawed Death there riding on the fuselage."

"Never mind him, answered the Major; "hand over the tools. . . . Are we ready? . . . Then shoot a modest two bits."

"Faded," was O'Shaugnessy's only word, as he discarded a quarter without the flicker of an eyelash. With the practiced hand of the experienced chiropractor, Major Perelman shook the bones and laid out a pretty little seven on the lower wing.

"Shoot the works, sweetheart," he said coolly, preparing to roll again.

"Ho K.," responded George, throwing down a handful of coins. The dice kissed each other, shook with passion, and revealed another natural. George gritted his teeth and watched Perelman narrowly. The latter hesitated, then decisively threw down a fifty-cent piece. George paled.

"Major!" he asked, his voice shaking. "You mean—"

"Shoot four bits," said Perelman coldly. "All or

HAPPY DAYS BEFO' DE WAH

A Southern incident: "What have you named your newest child, Uncle Eben?" queried a scion of the Southern aristocracy of that person.

"Why," said the humorous old retainer, "we ban named him Bill 'count he allus is bilious."

"Well," said the scion, "I suppose you'd name him John if he had jaundice!"

The old man blushed under his heavy coat of tan.

any part of it. This ain't no mug's game."

"Gad!" said O'Shaughnessy with awe in his face. "No wonder the French call you Chou-Chou avec Les Croutons (Perelman the Fearless)!"

"Well?" asked the Major, his steely gray eyes glittering behind his flight goggles, "am I faded or ain't I?" Tiny beads of perspiration stood out on George's forehead and his lip trembled. Then he pulled himself together and flung down a half dollar. The two men sat shaking with agitation and aviation as the little teeth shook feverishly and came to rest with eleven cavities showing. There was an ill-suppressed sob from George and he stooped down and commenced untying his shoestrings.

Three days later a disheveled Irish aviator was picked up behind enemy lines clad only in a barrel and a pair of socks. He told a confused story about a battle in the clouds which his captors could not understand. When questioned about his uniform, he said that it had been shot away in the fierce hand-to-hand conflict. And far away in London, the gallant Major, recovering from a serious blow on his finger incurred while trying to hang a picture in his den, smiled grimly and cut another notch in his automatic.

Did luck always follow the intrepid Ameer of the Air? Read in next week's JUDGE how the agile Arrow of Albion outwitted the crusty old Deacon and showed up Mark Smallgood's plans to rob the orphanage!

Fellow who bought a house-boat, to take a good rest, annoyed by two catfish.

How to Be a Detective

*By "Old Sleuth" Perelman,
former associate of "Bulky Benny" Bernstein,
and one-time Scotland Yard operative*

Pick up any large metropolitan newspaper and glance casually down the column headed "Detectives Wanted." Then run your eyes through "Errand Boys Wanted." Now scan the section "Laborers Wanted" and after that, "Bookkeepers and File Clerks, Male." If you can find a job, you're either a liar or ten times as good as I am, boys; I have been looking for a good break for twelve years, and the only steady occupation I have is standing around in those long lines outside the Bowery soup joints. But this is neither here nor there.

There is a real need in this day and age for keen-witted detectives, and any young man who would like to earn Big Money will find it in the detective game. There are few professions as fascinating as that of being a plainclothes bull, and if you have cold, gray eyes, a false whisker and a shiny badge, you too can tune in on "Station M-O-N-E-Y."

There are three kinds of detectives: smart detectives, dumb detectives and detectives. The first kind is found only in books by T.S. Fletcher and Sir Arthur Conan Doyle, so they can be dismissed without a word. Now how would a man go about being either a dumb detective or a detective? Let us see.

The first thing a detective must know are the clues. If no crime has been committed, there are generally no clues to the criminal. But sometimes a criminal will leave behind him some important trace of his identity, like his calling-card or his passport photo. If he leaves his card or his photo, the case is simple and all you have to do is find him. Come, we shall track down this fellow together.

First, we got to the nearest cigar store and inquire of the clerk whether he has recently sold a package of Luckies. After a moment's thought, he will tell you that he sold one some day last week to a mysterious individual with black, beady eyes and a satchel full of currency of large denominations. Now consult your Rogues' Gallery... aha! Here is our man sure enough! " 'Green Goods' Rogan, quick on the draw, smokes Luckies because he wants to safeguard his singing voice, graduate of Dannemora and Joliet Prep, fond of taking in washing." The rest is detail; simply insert a small ad in the personal column of any newspaper requesting men with black, beady eyes, packages of Luckies, and satchels full of currency to report to the nearest police station if they want to learn something to their advantage. In three days your quarry will have unsuspectingly walked into the trap.

"Say, Crepuscle, these ancient Hebrews sure know their stuff."

"Howzat, Kindred?"

"Oh, they were all to the manna born."

Sometimes clues are puzzling. I remember being assigned to cover a mysterious bank robbery in Hingham, Mass. The culprit had left behind nothing but an address book and some laundry bills with his name on them. Knowing that criminals always return to the scene of the crime, I waited patiently until my man stole back to recover his laundry bills, and then clapped the "bracelets" on him. Unfortunately he turned out to be the janitor cleaning up waste paper, but we later discovered the real offender, a hardened old miscreant named Bleach or Ledbetter or something, who used to beat his mother and steal brass rings from carnivals. He was quickly tried and found not guilty with extenuating circumstances. I hear he has gone South and is in the shell game, dredging for oysters in the Delaware Water Gap. 'Cess to you, Old Man, and don't let your newfound prosperity make you forget your old

JUST IN TIME

OR HOW THE WIDOWS AND ORPHANS WERE SAVED

Can you tell me where to buy an Angora? I need a cat that's a good Mauser. Wait, don't hit me till you've heard this: A sculptor I know was working on a statue of Melancholy. "And what are you doing there?" probed a friend. "Oh, just cutting a sorry figure!" snapped Epstein verbally. You can go now, Perelman, it's five o'clock.

WHO SAID THAT TENNIS WAS A SISSY'S GAME?

Well, gents, today's big turf super-special is Laddie-Boy Perelman in the fifth at Lincoln Fields, so play him on the nose to win, place, and show. Speaking of the whippets reminds me of the one about the two hoboes. Said Weary Williams: "I got a shock from a live wire today; gee, what a funny feeling, just like taking a bath!" "Good G—d!" replied Languid Lewis. "What a memory you must have!" Stand back, boys, a woman has fainted!

classmates in good old DeWitt Clinton!

Remember, this is only the first of a fatiguing series on Crime and Criminals. Ask your barber or dentist to reserve your copy containing the next big-value article "Which (Witch) Hazel?"

A Tip to the Radio Boys

The trouble with the radio, men, is that the advertising they send over it is too subtle. What's the use of having Begbaum's Blue Blowers play "Down on the Delta" and then follow it up with the announcement that if your feet hurt you, Topoozian's Trim-Phit Dog Guards will ease the pain? Answer, no use. There's no connection between the two. But if you wove Topoozian's and-so-forth into the song you'd get something pleasing to the ear and utilitarian at the same time. Like for instance:

"Down on the delta they're dancing with joy,
They're shaking that thing, and many a boy
And many a girl are blessing the name
And the fame of good old Topoozian, the same
Who sells his excelsior quality Dog Guards
At 543 Bergen Avenue, Jersey City, telephone Pinchbeck 4087."

That's what big-time ad men call Breaking Down the Consumer Resistance, and after you boys have heard that song a few times and begin to ponder on your feet, you'll probably take a cab to Ernie Topoozian's Corn Kennel and sink seven dollars in a pair of Dog Guards.

Or take the plays they broadcast over the radio. Why can't the playwright sneak a hidden allusion to the product right into the drama? It's a pipe. Look here:

FALTERING FEET
A Human Drama in 1 Act

Characters: Henry Tregaskis; Dollie LaRue, his fiancee; Muffin, a butler.

Scene: Library of Henry Tregaskis.

Tregaskis—I can't stand this any longer. I'm going away tonight—to Paris, Vienna, Yokahama—anywhere, as long as I can forget.

Muffin—Sir, a lady to see you.

Tregaskis (starting)—A lady! Who can it be, Muffin?

Muffin—Just a broken thing, sir, a gay moth whose wings were singed in the flame men call Broadway—in short, sir, Miss D. LaRue.

A wag recently said to Smith, "Jones, I should hate to be as short as you." "Why?" asked the end man. "Because when you are ill, you don't know whether you have headache or corns!" was the reply, quick like a whip. The confusion of Jones was comical to see.

Tregaskis—Send her in and—Muffin!

Muffin—Yes, sir.

Tregaskis—You may take the evening off—I shan't need you again to-night.

Muffin—Very good, sir.

Dolly (entering)—Sweetheart!

Tregaskis—Loved one!

Dolly—Why are you so thoughtful, buglets? Have you perhaps suffered reverses in a financial way or are you unwell?

Tregaskis—Dolly, I have a confession to make to you.

Dolly—Henry! Have you been keeping something or somebody from me?

Tregaskis—Yes, Dolly, but now I must tell you. I am going away to forget.

OH BOY JUST GIVE A LOOK AT THESE 2 NIFTY MAMMAS

Two Wall Street brokers were chatting over their toast and milk one day. "Thank God, times have changed!" exclaimed the elder, a tall distinguished man with a striped hat band. "Why?" asked his junior. "Ah, just think of wearing stocks around your neck as they did in the old days!" was the apt retort. They both shook with ill-concealed mirth.

Dolly—But Henry, what have I done, what have I done?

Tregaskis—It is no fault of yours, child. My feet hurt, and I shall find oblivion on foreign shores.

Dolly (tearfully)—Don't leave me, darling, oh, my darling.

Tregaskis (firmly)—I must. The trouble I'm having with my feet, you wouldn't believe it if I told you.

Dolly (suddenly)—Henry, I can help you!

Tregaskis (incredulously)—You?

Dolly—Yes, me. Have you ever heard of Ernie Topoozian of 543 Bergen Avenue, Jersey City?

Tregaskis—No.

Dolly—He is the man who can relieve your feet pains! Aching swollen bunions, and tired listless corns respond over-night to his treatment. For seven dollars he will sell you a pair of Topoozian's Imperial Trim-Phit Dog Guards, warranted to ease your suffering.

Tregaskis—If this is true, Dolly, I say if this is true, it means that we will begin life all over again, anew!

Dolly—It is true, Henry, or you get your money back!

Tregaskis—Thank God that there was a woman's sympathetic hand and feminine intuition to lead me back to the light!

Dolly—Darling!! (They embrace.)

CURTAIN.

Scientists Agape as Savant Demonstrates New Cure for Hair Ills

New York, Dec. 15.—Arriving yesterday on the *Leviathan* and cheered by an enthusiastic crowd of bald-headed men and women, Dr. Fritz von Perelman, renonwned Austrian hair surgeon, was greeted by Grover Whalen and taken to the Hotel Mange, where he was interviewed by reporters. The eminent hair-specialist, before whose feet the dandruff world has fallen, was all smiles, despite the fact that he had been fearfully boiled for three days on shipboard.

"I am glad to be wiz you," he stated in a reply to queries, "and now bring on your American women." The doctor, who is a tall, distinguished man of twenty-four and completely bald, was immaculately dressed and wore on his bosom various important orders he had received. One was for a stein of beer

Figure 1

Figure 2

Figure 3

Figure 4

and a sandwich in a hurry, while another was for roast spring lamb with mint jelly.

Professor von Perelman has been carrying on his experiments for almost fifteen years, he told reporters. He was treating guinea-pigs for revelry in 1911 when quite by accident he noticed that five drams of Ron Bacardi in a glass of hot water produced a warm and comforting sensation.

"This was the basis of my first experiments," continued the famous specialist. "Later I found that by adding seven to ten drams, more desirable effects were secured. In a short time I found that the hot water was detrimental to the system, and I discarded it."

Some of the professor's miracle cures can be understood best by a glance at the accompanying photographs from his private collection. In Figure 1 we see a Mr. Lorentz, a Dutch contractor who had lost his hair from fright when a bar was closed at midnight. Note that in this picture Mr. Lorentz, in addition to being entirely bald, is also smooth-shaven. Figure 2 shows Mr. Lorentz after three months of the Ron Bacardi treatment. Not only has he grown a crop of wavy nut-brown hair, but his face is obscured by a curly and luxuriant beard. An odd feature of this case is the fact that he also grew a wing collar and black bow tie.

Figures 3 and 4 are perhaps the most startling examples of the noted savant's treatment. The first is a photograph of Mr. Ira Kapstein taken shortly after his gums had begun to recede and also his hair. Both his forehead and his chin had receded some time before, but he had thought nothing of it. Finally he consulted the professor and was treated with specially powerful injections of Ron Bacardi. Figure 4 reveals the sweeping changes wrought by Dr. von Perelman's panacea. The marvelous specific tightened up the sagging face muscles and lengthened the hair; it changed the patient's voice from a feeble soprano to a bull bass, and it grew a potted palm behind his left ear, as shown clearly in the photo.

Phantoms of the Dawn

The thrilling narrative of the Czar of Chicago's Underworld, "Diamond Sid" Perelman, acknowledged leader of the notorious "Loop Phantoms" mob and internationally known con man, safe-blower, and jewel connoisseur.

Editor's Note—After two years of negotiation with the authorities of Illinois, we have at last secured permission to present to the world for the first time this intensely human document, the story of the operation of the greatest criminal of all time, the formidable "Diamond Sid" Perelman, variously referred to as "The Scourge of Headquarters" and "The Man of a Thousand Faces." The deeds of Dick Turpin, Jonathan Wild, Gerald Chapman, "Silver Bob" Van Roosa and "Golden Mein" Anthony read like nursery couplets beside this enthralling recital, with its dizzying climaxes in ACTUAL drawn battles with the minions of the law. But let the story speak for itself.

CHAPTER 1

A circle of white excited faces closed in around "Bloodhound" McGonigle, head of Chicago's plain-clothes squad. The crowd grew; men and women craned their

The swift grey Phantom of the Dawn has struck again!

necks to peer into the center of the crush. McGonigle, burly, gray at the temples, a cigar in his teeth, straightened up suddenly and turned to a bystander.

"What did you see?" he asked in clipped accents, whipping out a leather notebook.

"Yeh," replied the onlooker intelligently, "Me no spik Englis, fella."

"You'll get six months for this, you dog!" said McGonigle heatedly. "Take him away, Morrissey." And turning to another bystander, he ground out,

"Come clean now! What did you see?"

"I saw a little guy with a can opener fooling around that gum machine," was the reply.

"And then?" asked McGonigle.

"I can't say," replied the poor apple. "The next thing I knew there was a red haze in front of my eyes and when I came to I saw the little guy heave away a flock of pennies, grab a handful of gum, and run. That's all, mister, and now I gotta go; my wife's waiting for these spuds."

The police photographs of the gang leader, revealing his ability to change his features at will.

The crowd waited tense as McGonigle closed his notebook with a snap and re-lit his cigar.

"Well, boys," he said to two respectful subordinates. "The Swift Gray Phantom of the Dawn has struck again. Somewhere in the tangled web of crime 'Diamond Sid' Perelman, the Eel of the Loop, smiles evilly as he recalls how he has just outwitted us."

All night long the mighty newspaper presses hummed and next day the wide-eyed man in the street read of the latest daring coup of the hooded Menace of Gangsterdom. And he, wily veteran of the underworld, smiled narrowly in his hideaway as he chewed gum endlessly. It was his perversion.

And now the scene shifts with startling rapidity to the first-class cabin of the steamer "Pride of Rivington Street," eight days out of Frisco, bound for Honolulu. Dinner is being served at the captain's table; a buzz of conversation hangs over the flawless napery and expensive cut-glass. Suddenly the captain, idly sipping soup, claps his hands to his breast and utters a cry.

"My God!" Stewards rush forward and passengers rise in alarm.

"What's the matter, Capt. Trotsky?" asks a tall distinguished diplomat.

"I've lost my fountain pen!" is the amazing retort as frightened women clutch at their jewels and men whisper excitedly. Suddenly a commanding voice is heard from the doorway. All turn; and there, framed like a dirty picture, stands McGonigle, chewing his cigar.

"It's no use, Captain," he says wearily. "Again the Law is powerless. The Man of a Thousand Faces has done his work well. Finish your soup."

And unbeknownst to all, twenty feet below the waterline in the furnace-room, a short man smiles to himself and plans. Yes, reader, it is none other than—Michael Dubowski, a Polish stoker from Scranton, and he is thinking of a peach of a story a little dame told him on the Barbary Coast.

When will the Asp of the Underworld strike again? What goes on behind the expressionless face of the Autocrat of the Gunmen?

See next week's chapter!

How to Prevent Snoring

I have been beleaguered of late with requests on how to curb snoring, several of them signed, "An Unhappy Wife," and one letter in particular from somebody who signs himself "Taxpayer." As there is nobody in the telephone book or the street directory by the name of "Taxpayer," I have come to the conclusion that this letter is a hoax and was sent by a man named either Hemmingway or Larkspur. I mention this purely to show that if Larkspur

CALL AT THE SERVANTS ENTRANCE MY GOOD MAN ORDERED "ISABELLE ICILY

SO THIS IS PARIS!

How pride can ofttimes take a fall is well brought out in a mighty funny story from Butte, Mont., sent in by Mrs. Daniel Harbowitz, of Atlantic Avenue. A farmer's son had been graduated from Harvard and arrived home full of his own importance. "Now that I'm a college graduate," he told his father, a Mr. Riskin, "I shall want a good field to demonstrate my talents in." His poppa looked him over and then said, "Wa'al, there's a ten-acre one over thar in thet corner which you can hoe. Raowdy-dow!" And he slapped his thigh in merriment. Needless to say, his son did not see the joke. Neither do we, to tell the truth.

thinks he has put one over on me, he will find a good sock in the breadbasket waiting for him if he cares to call at the office.

But I must be more gallant with the ladies, so shall endeavor to point out one or more ways to discourage this practice. Before I set down a standard recipe for snoring which has been in the family for three generations, I should like to tell a little story which is credited to Chauncey Depew and which concerns Eugene Field. Mr. Depew was on his way to Eugene Field one day to see Villanova play Loyola when he encountered a small boy. The tot informed Mr. Depew that his teacher had allowed her class to take the afternoon off. "Why, hasn't she a substitute?" asked the great man kindly. "No, she has a sick headache," was the tot's response. This is a good story to quiet people suffering from sick headaches and can also be used to provoke same.

According to the Jewish Encyclopedia, snoring is an old vice and goes back to the Chaldeans, who built many good roads, some of which still exist. Speaking of the Chaldeans reminds me of two friends of mine who are great wise-crackers and are a couple of cards. Like the other day Thurber said to Rausch, "Do you know what Jewish ice-cream is?" "Sure, ice-cream Cohens (cones)!" says Rausch just like that. So Thurber says, "You must drink constantly." And Rausch says, "No, I drink whiskey!" Well, Thurber says, "Is your nose red like that all the time?" and Rausch says, "No, it is red like that until I blow it and then it is blew (blue)!" Then Rausch says, "You look like you have a bad cold; what are you doing for it?" "Coughing!" says Rausch like a flash. "Well, I don't feel well either," says Thurber. "I got hit in the synagogue." "Where was that?" says Rausch. "In the temple!" says Thur-

LEARN TO PLAY THE HARP!!
EASY! PROFITABLE! UNCANNY!

"What do you consider the first requisite in business?" inquired Smithers of his friend Serime, who deals in goose feathers. "Pluck," retorted the latter, his eyes twinkling merrily. The first speaker's jaw dropped in chagrin.

ber. "Say, where are you from?" asks Rausch. "I am from Providence," says Thurber. "Are you?" says Rausch. "No, R.I.!" says Thurber. "Well," says Rausch, "I used to know a landlady there who ran off with one of her boarders." "No," says Thurber, "that was only a roomer (rumor)!" Those two boys are certainly clever. They can go on like that for hours.

Well, I see where I have used up my time, so I will now sum up and leave our side to the decision of judges. Resolved, that the Philippines should have their independence, because the U.S. no longer needs them for a coaling station.

Ladies and gentlemen, honorable judges, and worthy opponents, I thank you.

Not-So-Indian Love Call

Some guy in a speakeasy the other morning was broadcasting a line that this Lost Tribe of Israel you all heard about was really the Sioux or the Blackfeet or one of those Indian tribes, that they had ferried themselves over from Asia Minor and become absorbed into our great Melting Pot. Well, this looks like maybe there was a grain of truth in it, so I have taken a little plot out of a stamp-album and bedecked it with fantasy for children of all ages from seven to seventy. So order a shampoo from your barber and start right in.

NOT-SO-INDIAN LOVE CALL
A Simple Tale of Love Among the Not-So-Redmen

Night was falling over the Morton Rosenberg Mutual-Benefit-and-Protective-Budget-Plan-Reservation. Everywhere campfires gleamed between the brightly painted teepees. Here and there a squaw was pounding corned beef or salami for the evening meal, while husky braves squatted in groups and went into bankruptcy. Outside the great tent of Morton Rosenberg, Grand Sachem of the tribe, two young warriors, Pay-While-You-Play Levine and You-Furnish-the-Squaw-We-Furnish-the-Wigwam Feinberg, stood guard.

Inside the teepee the wily old sachem and his chief medicine-man, Dignified-Credit Schossman, drowsed over the council pipe. Suddenly the flap of the tent was thrown open and Snaky Shirley Rosenberg, the fairest daughter of the venerable chief, stood revealed.

"Nu, this is a hell of a time to come busting into a tent!" exclaimed the sachem aggrievedly. "Where was you all afternoon?"

GO, BASE VILLAIN, AND NEVER DARKEN THESE DOORS AGAIN

"Say, guy, did you have much trouble when you started in growing your moustache?" asked a young lady of a much bewhiskered boy friend.

"Yes," replied he laughingly, "I often felt down in the mouth."

"Listen, poppa," said Shirley sweetly, "I think you're gonna have a son-in-law at last. I gotta proposal from a guy."

"From another one of those pool-sharks?" asked her father. "I should start supporting some loafer that he wears Slickit on the hair and sheik

THE SCORE IS FORTY "LOVE" SAID FRANK MEANINGLY

"Most of the action of my story takes place in a cemetery," an author is reported to have told a fair friend of his. "Well," said the demure girl, throwing him a roguish glance, "isn't that the best possible place for a plot?" Both of them had a good laugh at this, and linking arms, they adjourned to the bar.

clothes? Listen, you—''

"Why, poppa!" objected Shirley, "this ain't no pool-player! This is Money-Refunded-and-Satisfaction-Guaranteed Ginsberg!"

"Oy!" gasped the chieftain, "that cheap soda-jerker! My only daughter in love with a soda-fountain! A Rosenberg married to a raspberry float! Over my dead body!"

As he spoke the tent-flap was again lifted and a tall young brave, with a quiver full of Arrow collars, entered.

"Here you are!" growled Rosenberg. "So you want to marry MY daughter, hey? With your prospects? What you'll be supporting her on, banana splits? Phooy!"

"Now listen, chief," remonstrated Ginsberg. "I gotta new racket, and if you wanta get in on the ground floor, we'll have our name in lights on Rivington Street yet!"

"What is it, good-for-nothing?" queried Rosenberg. "But, mind you, I ain't listening!"

"All right, Mr. Rosenberg," replied the young brave. "Here: I got a swell scheme. Why shouldn't you and me handle a little sideline of classy Indian blankets for carnivals and fairs? We'll get the blankets on consignment, and you'll be the Western sales manager. I got maybe two, three thousand dollars laid away—"

"Say, what did you say your name was again?" asked Rosenberg. "Maybe a smart young feller like you—if I was to put in my business experience—so drop in in the morning and we'll give it a *schmoos!*"

The slim young Indian brave and the girl lifted the flap of the tent and walked into the circle of gleaming fires.

"Oh, Austin!" said Shirley tenderly, "I knew he'd love you as soon as he saw you! And we'll have a little home in the Dyckman section and maybe a cottage at Far Rockaway— oh, AUSTIN!"

"Sure, and we'll name the first papoose The-Home-of-True-Values Ginsberg, darling!" murmured Austin softly as Shirley hid her blushing face. "Just wait Shirley dear, I'll buy you a diamond that it'll make Mount Monadnock look like a wart, sweetheart!"

And, hand in hand, they walked into Silverman's Sandwich-and-Bar-Rail toward the beginning of a new dawn.

Female Detective—*He's a cad, a bounder, a wretch and a mean old thing!*
Mrs. Axminster—*Why, Sylvia, what's this all about?*
Female Detective—*I'm running down a criminal.*

Are You Going Away This Summer?

Many an otherwise charming fellow has been struck dumb the whilst sojourning in Vacationland when the merry party of which he is a unit asks him if he can rope and tie a steer. There has been a flush of interest this season in "The Sport of Kings," as roping and tying the bovines is termed, so I have compiled a few hints that they will fit right in your grip with the pemmican and the saltines and maybe save you that hot flash of embarrassment.

What kind of steers are there? is your first query. Well, two kinds, I should say, good and bad. Like, for instance, one day last winter I got a telephone

QUICK WATSON THE NEEDLE MUTTERED HOLMES IN A WHISPER?

There have always been a lot of "Wise Crashers" down in good old Far Rockaway, but Sherlock Holmes (age twelve, 174 Beach Boulevard) is the "Wisest." Said he to a friend recently, "I hit father with my car the other day." "Well, father was getting on," rejoined the boy friend. "I know," shot back Sherlock, "but I crumpled the mudguard!" Wasn't that a honey of a reply?

call that she claimed she was a blonde just in from the "Windy City" and feeling lonely, so would I come up to her apartment on the Drive and while away a rainy afternoon? Being an unmarried man and having seen all the movies in town, I accepted the offer. It turned out later that her spouse was a traveling man, a chap named Al Horn, who was in the tinware and adventure-stories game down in Capetown. There was a strange sequel to the episode, as it chanced he blew in suddenly from Africa, and there being no closets in the apartment, why I spent the night on a tin roof, which it wouldn't be so bad only there was a cold sleet driving down at the time, and I had left the young lady's flat without my vest and jacket. I mention this simply as an example of a bum steer.

Most roping and tying of steers is done with the aid of small ponies or pintos. To get familiar with these creatures, I would follow these directions: You first make a good breakfast of clinical thermometers and then take the subway and ride to 155th Street. Then change to a local and get off anywhere along the line. This process is called "visiting the broncs" and it will be good practice in associating with animals.

Now that you have familiarized yourself with roping and tying the steers, the next question is how to rope the calves. The best quality twine should be used and the knots should be adjusted so that there is no strain on the instep. "Langworthy" (the medical name for strain on the instep) has washed away a good many people in their prime, so better see a physician if you are not up to snuff. The healthy adult should be up to snuff at least three times during the coming semester or know the reason why.

Incidentally, the writer saw a little news item in the paper the other day about a hen, that these cats' mother had died so the biddy adopted the pussies and reared them. What do you think of that for the wonders of modern science, and I guess this is an answer to the atheists and scoffers. America has no room in their midst for people who are always tearing down our national institutions and ideals, and if they can't shut up, then let them go the hell back where they came from. We have no use here for these "Bolshevists," and, anyway, how would you like your own sister to be nationalized? Besides, they never take a bath, so there you are.

In conclusion here is a small poem that my brother in primary school had left over from writing an epic, so seeing we are on the subject, I will let you see how it runs:

"Roping the Steers on the Texas Range"

Oh, leap in your saddle and whip up the bronc,
You don't need no Klaxon for you to cry Honk! Honk!

HER FIRST COTILLON WITH DASHING BRUCE GINSBERG

TALK IS CHEAP

Here is a good laugh on the commuter. Little Hubert Parks was on the ferry with his mother. Suddenly he nudged her, and pointing to a lady who sat nearby, inquired, "Who's that, mumsey?" "Why, that is a Sister of Charity, dear," replied the clever housewife. "Which one, mumsey, Faith or Hope?" shot back Hubert. This filthy little wise-cracker got what he deserved.

HAVING A BARREL OF GOOD CLEAN FUN?

A good book is ofttimes a much better holiday present than a jackknife, as the following "wheeze" shows. Mrs. Minkowitz, 1524 Grand Concourse, asked her son, "Tell me, Robin, have you ever seen a burial at sea?" Robin gave her a warning look and replied, "No, but during one trip I took to Europe, there was a wake all the way over." Mrs. Minkowitz visits Robin every day in the hospital and brings him fruit and flowers.

Out there in the ranges so free, just you and me
And that baby calf makes three,
Who's wonderful? Who's marvelous I hear
It's that there Texas longhorn steer,
So rope him and tie him and ride with a vim
Over there to the edge of the great Tonto Rim;

Chorus:
So hurrah for the girls of New Haven,
Hurrah for the streets that they roam,
Hurrah for the rings that they carry,
God knows but they may be your own!

Are You a "Good Skate"?

With the temperature at 107 degrees in the shade and twelve people carried feet first into Bellevue this morning, suffering with sun-stroke, there is no time like the present to begin thinking about fancy and figure skating next winter. True, there are plenty of you who will be "skating on thin ice" this summer, going out with married women—ha, ha, ha—but seriously, that is another kind of skating and deserves a whole book by itself. Sometimes I hope to write this book, and what a book it will be, oh, boy, oh, boy, OH, BOY!

First for a little history of "The Sport of Kings" (skating). Skates were invented by two Dutch process-servers named Lewis Cockroft and Pablo Picasso around 1850. They worked in relays for three days, at the end of which time Cockroft had perfected a left-hand skate and Picasso a right-hand one. Picasso later invented the microscope and revolving doors, but died of a sudden writ of replevin. Cockroft, on the other hand, emigrated to France and became the leader of the Cubists, a gambling and dice organization. So much for the history of skates.

THERES BAR IN THEM THAR
MOUNTINGS MUTTERED PIERRE

PAUL, THE PEDDLER, OR BOUND TO WIN

If this one doesn't give you a toothache, nothing will. The scene is a busy newspaper office. On all sides one hears the hum of typewriters and the swish of paste pots. Enters Gillooly, a young cub reporter. "Chief, where will I put this account of the man who fell and broke his back?" he asks the city editor. "Why, in the spinal column, of course" replies the witty journalist. Is it any wonder that newspapermen drink?

The most difficult branch of "the finny sport" (skating) is undoubtedly figure skating. Apropos of the latter, an amusing anecdote cries aloud to be told. A well-known figure in the world of sport in five letters, meaning "incapable of refusing strawberries," had been a fancy skater for years. His specialty was forming figure eights on the ice. Tiring of the simplicity of figure eights, he began to form figure sixteens, figure thirty-twos, and eventually figure sixty-fours. From this it was only a step to figure one-hundred-twenty-eights, figure two-hundred-fifty-sixes and figure five-hundred-twelves. At present this noted skater is engaged in cutting figure one-hundred-thirty-one-thousand-seventy-twos at Baffin Bay, the only place large enough for the purpose. His ankles have long since disappeared and are replaced by early colonial day-beds, named Perry Schwartz.

No doubt you have seen skating exhibitionists pick up their female partner and whirl her around, holding her by the leg, and wondered how it was done.

There are several ways to pick up a female partner, one of them by driving up to the sidewalk and saying, "Hello, cutie, are you walking up my way?" but be careful that she is not a policewoman. Another way is to disguise yourself as a masseuse in a woman's Turkish bath—that is, if you want a Turkish girl friend—but pick out one that is not above the second story, as you may have to leave by the window. A friend of mine who thought that his girl friend was unmarried had to jump—but here we are getting off the subject again.

The hardest feat in figure skating is the crull. To be a good cruller ranks with being able to eat a banana under water and graduating from night school with honors. Even more difficult than the plain crull is the Australian crull. My advice to anybody who wants to be a cruller is to coat themselves with brown sugar and plunge in hot fat for ten minutes. Then garnish with parsley, sprinkle with lemon butter, and give yourself up.

Well, girls, I think I hear Dementia calling me from the garden, so I guess I will put on my bee-keeper's veil and "run along." As a little parting present from the author to you, here is a "good one" about bees he just made up all out of his

"JOE" "AL"

NOW THATS WHAT I CALL A PRETTY NIFTY PARCEL SAID JOE

Here is a good way to tell the difference between a duck and a tiger. Two policemen met one evening. "Rafferty," said one, "that man you arrested yesterday was deaf as a post. He didn't know you were arresting him." "That's all right, Cushman, answered the acute bobby, "he'll get his hearing before the judge!" These two wags should have gone on stage.

own head:

Husband—Well, I just bought a hive of bees at a bargain!

Wife—You may think it was a bargain, but I bet you "got stung"!

Good News, Tariff-Lovers!

This morning whilst I was busying myself in our sunny kitchen cleaning and singeing myself an old feather boa for lunch, I heard the postman's cheery whistle outside. Quickly dusting the flour from my hand, I opened the door.

"Now, Roy, how many times have I told you not to kiss me whilst my husband is in the house?" I rebuked, "Jest supposin' he should walk in and find us here in flagrante delicious?"

"Tush, Freda, don't scold!" he interrupted wilfully, boy that he is, "I just couldn't help it! What do you think? The new Hirschberg-Snedecker tariff bill is here!" I uttered a joyful cry and together we stripped the wrappings from the package he had brought. What fun! Two hours later, when Bert came up from his boats and things, we were still sitting in rapt delight thumbing over the clauses and provisos.

The Hirschberg-Snedecker tariff is named after its two sponsors, Fabius Bamberger and Rudy Vallee, both Congressmen from the Fourth Ward, which is bounded on the north by Evans Street, on the south by Pratt Street, and the east and west by Fox's Book of Martyrs. The text of the tariff is so familiar to all voters that repeating it would only cause you a severe case of phlebotomy or peristalsis. But there are two or three important changes this year so dull that it would be criminal to overlook them.

Article 17 of the tariff prohibits Armenians from bringing in gloves like that shown in Fig. 1. As a matter of fact, it also prohibits Armenians, but this is beside the point (that is, Armenians are beside the point). The truth is that these gloves, bristling with spines, have been sneaked into the country for use

BE AN ARTIST! MAKE BIG MONEY!

"My uncle left me out of his will, curse it!"

"Well, why can't you contest it, Reuben?"

"I can't, not until he's dead."

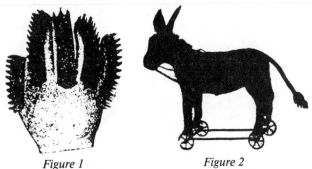

Figure 1

Figure 2

in mock porcupine soup, and the real porcupine soup interests have been forced to the wall. Many a man, licking his chops in anticipation of a tasty porcupine soup, has suddenly discovered one of these gloves awash in his plate instead of the jagged delicacy he expected. So down with the cheap foreign substitute and let our slogan be *"Native porcupines for America's dinner table!"* or failing that, *"Porcupines with first citizen's papers for America's dinner table!"*

Then there is the hollow wooden horse ban. The people in the cellar grottoes of Troy, New York, have risen to the surface as one man and protested against the importing of hollow wooden horses of the type of Fig. 2. Again and again, they claim, they have granted permission to strangers to park a hollow wooden horse inside the city walls. Then, in the dead of night, a door in the horse's stomach opens, 300 valid Armenians issue forth, and before you can scramble into your pajamas, they have captured the city, stolen the sheep, and eaten the covenants out of

HELLO CENTRAL GIVE ME HEAVEN

The scene is a river bed; the characters, a father oyster and Hannah, his youthful daughter oyster. Said the father oyster: "Now, Hannah, I want you to behave yourself while I'm gone." "Ah, poppeh," replied the young one, "this is June, and nobody expects an oyster to be good at this season!" The old man's amusement knew no bounds.

the plum cake. ''What good is plum cake without covenants?'' cry the Trojans, ''Down with the swarthy Armenoid invader thundering at our gates!'' So when Article 31 of the Hirschberg-Snedecker tariff goes into effect, Troy will be persona non grotto and nobody home to the wooden equines.

The most important change of all, however, is Article 39. There are today in Holland over 45,000 boys stuffing leaks in the dike with their index finger. Every year thousands of new boys pour in looking for leaks to stuff and it has kept the Dutch engineers worn to a mere Bramwell boring holes for them. Article 39 provides that one-half of all new boys entering Holland be chopped up with parsley, mohair, and hard-boiled egg and used in overstuffed armchairs. The other half will be christened ''Arthur Schreiber'' and stowed away in transatlantic airplanes. In this way a substantial profit will be realized.

The only other thing new today is this matter of the catch on the bathroom door. I bet I have spoken to Mr. Baumgarten a hundred times about it, but does he do anything? No. Before I got through taking my bath yesterday I counted 46 people in the room, not including three Prussian uhlans. *This has got to stop.* So take note, Prussian uhlans: If bathe you must, please leave your horses in the foyer with the checkroom girl. How would you like to reach for the soap and find yourself nestling in a horse's armpit? I warn you, if this happens again, you and I are all washed up.

Yours very coolly,
Thyra Samovar Perelman

Chinese Bandits Kidnap Coolidge!

Sage of Northampton Held for Ransom by Fu-Manchu Agents!
by S.J. Perelman, Ransom Editor of JUDGE

Northampton, July 30.—Residents of Northampton cringe in dread tonight before the sinister menace of the Yellow Peril. The mysterious disappearance yesterday of Calvin Coolidge, local lawyer, has been definitely pronounced to be kidnapping by Alfred Dunhill, Northampton's stalwart chief of police.

''Mr. Coolidge was kidnapped by agents of Fu-Manchu,'' stated Capt. Dunhill, ''and it is my belief that he is being held for ransom in a blasted oak on Pratt Street. When I get hold of those Chinese, you can bet your life that I will make medium shrift of them.''

''What do you mean by medium shrift, Captain?'' I asked.

''I thought at first of making short shrift of them,'' was the answer. ''Then for a while I favored long shrift, but now I am compromising.'' To demonstrate his compromising ability, Capt. Dunhill gave a short exhibition of the art. He was at one time assistant professor of compromising at Vassar, and knowing this, we asked him what he thought of that school.

"If I wanted my daughter to learn how to tipple I wouldn't send her there," stated the sleuth. "You can lead a horse to Vassar but you can't make her drink!"

Capt. Dunhill's theory of the disappearance is a unique one. Police records show that for a time Coolidge lived in Washington, where he operated a billiard parlor. While there he was visited by a mysterious Oriental who sold him a valuable piece of medicated gauze which had been an heirloom in Buster Keaton's family.

"This gauze," elaborated Capt. Dunhill, "was the only piece of its kind in America. It had come into Keaton's possession when he had roodles as a boy."

"Roodles?' I queried in perplexion. "What are they?"

"While going to school Keaton suddenly began to grow a third set of fingers," explained Dunhill. "When doctors examined him, they announced that every third hand was roodles and ordered him to eat medicated gauze and cream."

Obviously this Chinese had stolen the gauze and was being trailed by the notorious Fu-Manchu gauze ring, for he was found floppo the next day in a deserted lot on the outskirts of the city. The fine Chinese hand of Fu-Manchu was immediately detected by secret service men. When Coolidge returned to Northampton, the previous gauze went with him. Fu-Manchu's agents thereupon rented the other half of Coolidge's two-family villa, bored holes in the connecting walls and in Coolidge, and listened. After five weeks of silence, they heard Mr. Coolidge say, "Maybe." Now was the time to strike.

"They posted a Chinese boy in front of the house," continued Dunhill. "He began to whistle 'On the Road to Mandalay Where the Flying Knishes Play'. Mr. Coolidge ran to the window and they seized him in a trice and bore him away."

"What sort of trice was used, Capt. Dunhill?"

"A Chinese trice," averred the bulldog of justice, "probably with copper handles and no rumble seat. And that's the last we've seen of him."

He had hardly concluded when Mr. Coolidge appeared in the doorway, attired in a fringed buckskin suit and Iroquois war-bonnet. As reporters crowded around him, he smiled slightly and immediately apologized for it.

"Well, boys," he said, "all I can remember is a red haze, and when I came to, there I was with the smoking pistol in my hand."

L'OVE'S' AWAKENING 'OR' SOMETHING LIKE THAT

The big laugh this week comes from Harriet Schmoltz of 44 Eastern Parkway, in the Bronx. Harriet and a boy friend were talking over fancy ways of dying, a good pastime for a hot day. Said Harriet: "Shure, and I'd rather be burned to death than be beheaded, Flanagan." "And why?" queried the little fellow. "Well, parried the maiden coyly. "Who wouldn't prefer a hot roast to a cold chop?" This nutty come-back drew tears to Flanagan's eyes.

"How is 'Red' Hayes?" asked one reporter eagerly. "I haven't seen him since he took off the deep end." He was quickly embalmed amid laughter and turned over to the deck steward for disposal.

Mr. Coolidge will be tried next Wednesday for shooting quails and will probably be found not guilty. His defense will be that the quails attacked him. Watch for JUDGE's account of the Coolidge Quail trial, appearing in an early issue.

The Escutcheon Knife Clinic

While everybody has been rending homage to Dr. Albert Einstein and laying bouquets of sweet peas, Guarnerius violins, and Berlin summer homes at his feet, another and more modest genius has been revolutionizing surgery in this country. The Fourth Dimension is all very well, but what about the man that only takes a drop now and then and is not a habitual drunkard? I do not like to be a flat wheel on the car of progress, but just wait till they try to enforce it. It is a dirty trick on our boys in the trenches and if I am elected I will see that each and every constituent receives a package of rice seeds to plant in their back yard and fight the yellow labor menace. I guess we Californians will not bow the heel to the swarthy Mongol invader, as how can you expect a college graduate with one-and-one-third children per capita to live on two cents a day? Why, friends, even a Zionist could not do it, let alone a white man.

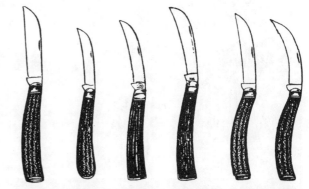

Sibyl Goldwasser during the six stages of meat-knife bend.

But let us get back to the Escutcheon Knife Clinic, founded last week on Pratt Street with money donated by John Escutcheon, a cartoonist on the South Bend "Tageblatt." As a young man Escutcheon had fallen in love with a capricious meat-knife, but she would not marry him.

"I am a career girl," she said stoutly, "and why should I give up my work in the abattoirs to scrub pots and pens for you? Please release your arms from around my shirtwaist."

"Then how about companionate marriage?" pleased John. "You could go back to the sheep-shambles and I could live with your folks."

"Any alliance between a Goldwasser and a cartoonist is infeasible," interrupted Sibyl stiffly. "Shall we rejoin the Breckenridges in the arboretum? They must wonder why we have been gone so long."

The blot of failure on Escutcheon drove him, a broken man, back to his easel in an attempt to forget. Years passed and, like all cartoonists, he amassed huge sums. Then one day he encountered Sibyl Goldwasser in a pecan grove. She was still the piquant Sibyl of other days but that bane of diseases, meat-knife spinal curvature, had bent her proud back. She whose elastic spine had graced South Bend's most brilliant binges now looked like a question-mark. Before Escutcheon could speak, she closed with a loud snap and doubled up at his feet. He pressed the spring in the small of her back and she smiled weakly as she unfolded. A moment later she succumbed in his arms with a sigh. Escutcheon was so moved that he dedicated his remaining years and the five dollars he had earned by cartooning to the eradication of meat-knife bend, as it is popularly called.

As you can see from the photographs—that is, if you are still reading this—the disease transformed Miss Goldwasser overnight from a healthy vivacious meat-knife surrounded by adoring boy-friends into an effete voluptuary, wearied of the gay life of European capitals, seeking solace in the momentary pleasures of the elusive absinthe. The last three stages show her holding the tell-tale noggin of absinthe while parasitic gigolos lounge about her in gray lounge suits. Gone is all her youthful elasticity, lubricity, and electricity, leaving two rooms and a bath which look as if the people that used to live there kept coal in it. Some people certainly are swines, taking the bulbs out of the sockets, breaking up the furniture, and jumping the lease with a phone bill of twenty-six dollars. No wonder Escutcheon refuses to sublet his apartment next summer.

In conclusion, nobody seems to have paid any attention to our last call for funds to carry on the good work. If every man, woman, and child who reads this will send us five dollars, we will have fifteen dollars, which is more than enough. Just shove your fiver in an envelope, mail it to Mr. Perelman in care of this magazine, and write it off to "Contributions" on your income tax. You will anyway, you chiseling cheapies.

AW GO FRY YOUR EARS SAID THE INDIGNANT PARROT

NEDDY'S APT RETORT

People are often given ether for serious operations, as this bully yarn well proves. A Mrs. O'Malley, of Ireland, was strolling through the garden with her two sons, Neddy (aged twelve) and Clara (aged twenty). "One swallow doesn't make a summer," remarked Mrs. O'Malley, who was fond of good clean proverbs. "No," responded Neddy, making a noise like a woodpecker, "but one frog often makes a spring!" The old suffragette broke down and wept when she heard her son's tart sarcasm.

A ROMANCE IN ROCKAWAY; OR, HOW LOVE CAME TO A LIFE-GUARD

Now here is a "jim-dandy" story we heard when we were on the road for Bluth Bros. & Garfinkle, Misses's Cloaks and Suits. A lawyer was trying a case one time when suddenly a portion of the floor fell in and three jurors disappeared. Here was a trying situation; but quick as a flash, Finklestein turned to the judge and exclaimed: "Fiat lux ad organum est pro caelo non disputare; sed in summo Augustam prohibere habemus!" The judge was so pleased at this ready retort that he heaped flowers and fruit on the victorious attorney, who was borne from the courtroom on the shoulders of his friends.

Confessions of a Baby Chick

Oh, Mr. Editor Mans, thank you so much for choosing me out of five hundred baby chicks to represent JUDGE at the National Poultry Show! After all, I am only a fuzzy little bundle of adorable white meat and I am afraid I shall feel so lost among all those distinguished aristocrats of poultrydom. I know that I am only a simple little country girl with no "fine feathers," but my motto is "handsome is as handsome does" and sometimes I think that it is better to wear calico and have your good name than to accept samples from lingerie salesmen and not know where your next husband is coming from. Like in the ballad:

"Rags! Rags! Rags!
On beautiful women and hags!
The rags for which someone demands heavy toll.
The price tag is plainly marked 'body and soul.'
The rags that mean heartache and sorrow and shame.
They're lovely and gorgeous—but rags just the same."

Don't you think that's so, Mr. Editor Mans? It was like I said when you were pressing my foot in the speakeasy, "No, Jack. I don't want your Jamaica rum and I don't want your Havana cigars; all I want is a little—respect."

But I must start the story of my life from the beginning. I first saw the light of day at Random, R.I. We were sixty-four girls and eleven boys, and Mamma, who was a No. 43-B model Schwartz-Feinberg incubator, was very vague about Papa. I believe he was an engine-wiper on the Atchison, Topeka and Santa Fe. She used to say that her trouble was that she had nourished a wiper in her bosom.

NOW, DONT PULL THE GAG ABOUT BEING SANTY CLAUS BROKE, IN SYBIL, WEARILY

FARM AND FIRESIDE

No kiddin', people, you can't beat them tots in Tottenville, Staten Island! Sally Gaffney, 3, was kibetzing around with Aaron Apple, 2, several days ago. "Does your father hang up his stocking Christmas Eve?" inquired Sally. "H—l no!" replied the little Apple, "but he hangs up the baker, the butcher, and the fruiterer!" They took Sally out feet foremost.

"Your father was a mountebank and a charlatan," she said coldly. I remember her taking us into the gun-room and showing us several cups he had won in a Charlatan contest in 1908 and a Black Bottom contest in 1909.

With Mother alone in the world, she had a hard time of it raising us and it took plenty of grit—over five pails, I learned subsequently. Whenever we used to pick on her, she would say helplessly, "I have to stand for plenty from you, you big brood!" But then the sunshine would appear through her tears and she would hum the theme song from "Point Counterpoint," "Point Counterpoint, I Love YOU." Mother has been chicken pie and fricassee these twelve years, but I still think of her.

When the time came for me to enter Bryn Mawr, my brothers and sisters, who were at their Wit's End, N.J., home, sent me a handsome traveling case, and three days later I arrived collect at the office of Dean Goossens. She introduced me to Irma, Birma, Firma, and Mirma, my new room-mates, five of

THE BOY WILL YET BE A GREAT ARTIST PREDICTED REMBRANDT CONFIDENTLY

TOO MANY GAY WINE SUPPERS

Let us imagine ourselves in the luxurious boudoir of an interior decorator. On all sides precious stones, rich fabrics, aromatic perfumes and letters from admirers. Raoul, a young interior decorator, is conversing with Marvin, also of the profession. "I understand you broke off your engagement, Marvin," says the idol of thousands. "Yes," pouts Marvin, "her complexion didn't match the wall paper in my den!" How did you enjoy this peep into an exotic career?

COULD YOU LEND A GUY A DIME FOR A CUP OF JAVA? INQUIRED THE MARTYR.

Here is the very deuce of a yarn sent in from the sticks by some crab-apple Eddie Cantor in Ioway. A couple of papas were discussing their children. "Yes, I let my little Rafael read Rabelais and the Decameron all the time," said one. "What!" exclaimed the other, "That indecent literature?" "Sure!" snapped back the first, "I gotta keep him away from the tabloids at any price!" And they shot Lincoln, just think.

the loveliest Biff Orphingtons I had ever seen. In a few hours I was encrusted with Epsilon salts and had become a member of the Delta Kappa Epsilon sorority.

The following week we held a big dance in Ezra Pound, to which even our Kaffir servants were invited. It was a wonderful moonlit night and the garden, with its myriad twinkling lanterns, was a magic isle set apart for me and my gigolo, Balthazar Siegel. As Balthazar held me in his arms and made proposals, I thought that I would swoon. Suddenly I heard Mate Starbuck cry out from the ship's waist.

"Stern for all your lives!" shouted Starbuck. "The dam is broken and the waters are coming down from Lahore!"

In the confusion that followed, Balthazar and I slipped from the halyards into the captain's jollyboat and cast adrift the painter. We gave him brushes, a palette, and turpentine, *and today that little boy is Maxfield Parrishberg.* Sometimes I wish we had not been so liberal with our art materials.

After three days of frightful starvation—have you ever been adrift in an open boat without fresh water and inhibitions with a white woman?—we were beginning to despair of our lives. Sharks were following our craft and offering to loan us money at 200 per cent. An albatross hung around our neck like a choker. Would the Great Spirit never send down the blessed rain?... Then came the monsoon, and a day later we sighted a Lenox Avenue Local bound for Port Washingstein with a cargo of nougats and hard centers.

Memories, memories! How they recall themselves in this dim attic faintly perfumed with lavender! With fluttering hands I place the beribboned letters back in the drawer and hobble downstairs. For Balthazar is calling me from the apiary, and it is time for tiffin. Au revoir, but not good-bye, my cute little goslings.

Plant a Garden and Help Win the War

Yesterday, whilst I was dallying amongst the hedgerows in my tobacco-stained Harris tweed with my sturdy blackthorn, puffing my faithful old briar stuffed with fragrant cavendish, I heard the bitter-sweet notes of my first thrush, that happy harbinger of summer. A hot thrush of emotion swept over me as the ever-memorable words of that sterling bard, James Whitcomb Levine, recalled themselves in all their poignancy:

"How would a Howard suit suit you?
Come over and try it on,
You can get suited in something that's nifty

And ready-to-wear at twenty-two fifty,
Believe me, a garment that's from the best of material,
We're losing money, I'm not kidding you."

Yes, gracious Dame Summer is beginning to beckon us to the wildwood and we shall soon be decking our hair with garlands and listing to Pan's pipes. Soon dainty farmerettes will be seen carrying hoes and rakes into the garden and rakes will be seen carrying farmerettes into the barn. It all seems lak everythin's wakin' an' stirrin', he murmured, his ears aglow and his toe awkwardly describing circles in the hot sand.

Now, what plans have you laid for your garden, "Mr. Average Suburbanite"? Are you going to load your table with fresh greens and succulent fruits or are you going to stick to the same old diet of salt hoss and potatoes that gave you scurvy last summer? By the way, how *did* you make out with that scurvy of yours? Ethel told my wife you traded it in for a case of the botts and got four dollars to boot (or rather, to bott). Wish you'd drop me a line soon, Fred, as I'm thinking of giving Ethel a case of the botts for our anniversary.

WHAT WILL THE TAX-PAYER SAY TO THIS?

Here's a rich one about the Spanish Inquisition. The scene is a cheerful torture chamber about forty feet underground. The characters are the chief inquisitioner and a gent named Alfred, who is about to become a martyr. Says the inquisitioner: "Well, Alf, we're gonna roast you next, but we'll leave the choice of having it done to you!" "Well, fella," says Alfred, "if it's all the same to you, you can burn me in effigy! So long! Pleasant dreams!" And he took the elevator up to the first floor.

Last year Albert Charles Swinburne, author of "Small Garden-Patches," made $7.45 with a fine asparagus bed named Bruce Bodkin. You can't go wrong on an asparagus bed, home gardener, and if you want "Dew Cumme Inne" to be a show place, here's your grift. Unfortunately, Swinburne's garden was later ruined by snails. When the place was opened, the management admitted only snails in formal clothes. At that time Rudy Vallee and his Connecticut Snails were playing there and casual snail trade behaved itself. Then a low foreign snail element crept in and before you knew it, the dive was simply crawling with all sorts of undesirables. But that is typical of Life and nobody should expect smooth snailing all the time.

Right now I've a dandy little garden leeking with reeks and radishes—pardon me, reeking with leeks and ladishes—well, anyway it's a dandy little garden just twittering with birds. What more charming nook than this for the tired office-worker to bury himself up to his neck in sand, cover his conk with an old tarpaulin, and dream? For those who generally rest this way, a rubber hose secreted in the mouth so that the water spurts out of one's ears makes a quaint revolving spray. Next week I will tell you about my two prize-winning Hubbard squashes. They are members of the Horowitz family of musical squashes which caused a sensation recently by riding a white horse down Evans Street in the nude. (That is, the squashes were in the nude, not the white horse.) She wore an afternoon tea gown of yellow voile with slashed gussets and carried a bouquet of nostalgias. Immediately after the ceremony the couple left for Bodes, Ill., where they will open a luminary. The best of wishes from the girls on the bakery counter, Mr. and Mrs. Rasputin!

The rest of your garden problems, such as winnowing and threshing your wife and selecting delicious grubs for your slug salads, I will also have to leave for another time, for I see Rupert crunching up the gravel path in front of our villa and I must run out and chide him. He always spoils his appetite crunching those paths between meals, the wilful boy. Ah, these men! Sometimes I think they are all boys at bottom and that the road to a man's heart is like an army traveling on its stomach.

GETTING GERTIE'S GARTER

Here's a hot one from the bar. Old Joe Garfangle of the 7th District Court was conversing with Al Burp of the 12th Superior. "Yes," he said, "that lawyer over there reminds me of necessity." "Of necessity? Why?" inquired Burp, opening a can of sardines and going out to the baker's for bread. "Because he knows no law!" thrust back the brilliant Garfangle, and the cause was won.

Daisy's Revolver

"Wake up, sleepy-head, have you forgotten what day this is?"

Daisy Babcock, aged nine, sat upright in bed and rubbed her sleepy blue eyes in astonishment. To think that on her birthday of all days she had overslept! Daisy's Mamma stood regarding her with quizzical mien, waiting for her bewildered daughter to collect her wits.

"Of course I know, mother dear!" she cried seizing Mrs. Babcock in a bear hug, "I am nine years old today!"

"I thought you would remember, darling," laughed her mother, "But hurry and dress, dear, for Daddy has a surprise waiting for you downstairs."

What could it be, wondered Daisy as she quickly donned her new white muslin pinafore. But her mother was adamant and refused to divulge the great secret. With pounding heart Daisy completed her toilet and sped hastily down three flights of stairs. Sure enough, there was Daddy waiting for her, his hands hidden mysteriously behind him. Daisy's heart was almost bursting with excitement. And when Mr. Babcock held out a beautiful big baby doll with gorgeous dark eyelashes and it said "Mamma!" to her, Daisy's exultation knew no bounds. She clung tightly to her Daddy and kissed him.

"Oh Daddy, you are so good to me!" she exclaimed, "I am afraid a naughty girl like myself does not deserve such a pretty doll!"

"Tush, tush," said Mr. Babcock gruffly, dashing away a suspicious moisture from his eye. "That is not all Daddy has for you, darling." And he handed Daisy a thrilling package bound with blue ribbon and marked "From Daddy and Mummie to Daisy." Pink with impatience, Daisy tore open the box and discovered a lovely glass revolver filled with small orange, crimson,

OLD HARVARD, MOTHER OF MAN

Remember the old days at Harvard? The banjo players, fellows strolling arm in arm across the yard, soft songs in the twilight, the gin parties? Gone, all gone. But here is a story to evoke old memories. One of the professors asked in a classroom one day, "Freddie, how do you spell 'ice'?" "I-c-e!" answered Freddie readily. "Good, and now what is 'ice'?" queried the man of learning. "Why, it's water that fell fast asleep!" parried the witty sophomore, and his admiring classmates cheered him with a will. It takes a Harvard man every time to save the day.

LEARN THE ART GAME! FUN! PROFIT! FAME! BANANA OIL!!

The big value pork pie this week certainly goes to little Teddy, only eighteen months old. "How do you like Mamma's new silk dress, Teddy?" inquired his mother. "It's swell," replied Ted briefly. "And just think, Teddy, all this silk was provided by a poor little worm!" mused the good woman. "Are you referring to papa?" asked Teddy artlessly. Pretty raw one, hey, boys?

black, and white candies! Oh what fun they had that morning when Daisy and her Daddy played Wild West Indian all over the living-room! They were so absorbed that Mrs. Babcock had to call them to dinner three times before they realized that the whole morning had flown by.

All through the meal Daisy could not wait to return to her new toy and even ice-cream, a dish of which she was very fond ordinarily, received scant notice from her. She was scarcely through her dessert when Alicia Bismarck, her bosom chum who lived next door, arrived with a cake her mother had baked with nine red candles on it and "Best Wishes to Daisy" in icing across the top. All afternoon they played cowboy on the floor of Daisy's bedroom and their merry shrieks of laughter resounded throughout the entire house.

But all good things come to an end sooner or later, and at seven o'clock Mr. Babcock's dreaded command "Time for little girls to be in bed!" informed Daisy that her birthday was over. Both her Daddy and Mummie helped tuck her in bed and kissed her good-night. As Daisy felt her sleepy lids closing under the Sandman's gentle touch, the downstairs door closed and she knew that her parents had gone to the movies for the evening.

How long she slept Daisy did not know but she was awakened by the stealthy noise of feet in the hall below. It could not be her father or mother for she knew their footsteps by heart. Courageously she crawled out of bed and silently opened her door. There in the half-light stood a tall masked form with a bag over its shoulder. *It was a burglar!* He started violently when he beheld Daisy's nightgowned figure before him, and her next words were even more startling.

"Hands up!"

"What's that?" inquired the stunned burglar.

"I said hands up!" repeated Daisy firmly. In her fist was the glass revolver she had received as a birthday gift that morning. In the darkness it gleamed like

ROOM FOR IMPROVEMENT

We found this one in a shoe-shine parlor, so we had it dry-cleaned and here it is. Poor old Geebick had been hitting the flask for several hours before his marriage and when the time came for the ceremony he was pretty well fried. After the marriage the minister said to the bride: "How could you come to the altar with a man in that condition?" The bride bit off another hunk of candy and replied: "Say, fella, do you think I could have got him to come here if he was sober?" This dry retort certainly made the bridesmaids titter.

a real weapon. For a moment the burglar regarded her pityingly.

"What do you think you've got there?" he asked at last.

"A revolver," replied Daisy after some thought.

"Let's see it," replied the burglar. Daisy dutifully handed it to him and he examined it minutely. Then he surveyed Daisy even more minutely.

"Well," he said at last. "What did you think you were going to do with it?"

"I—er—I read a story in a book about a little girl who captured a burglar with a fake pistol," stuttered Daisy, "I thought it might work with you."

"Your trouble, little girl," advised the burglar kindly as he picked Daisy up and threw her over the banister, "is that you read the wrong books." And Daisy, who was floating swiftly down three flights of stairs, was in no mood to contradict him. The burglar then lit a cigarette and calmly began packing up the silverware.

And there, boys and girls, let us leave him. When they took Daisy out of the plaster three weeks later, the first thing she did was to reach up and hang one on her father's lug which bloomed there for many a day. As her mother started back in surprise she took a kick in the sweetbreads from her daughter which put her on the retired list for keeps. And from that day to this the only thing Daisy gets from her folks is fruit-cake.

For Rent—Thirty-Room Apartment, No Baths

Last week's shake-up in the banking biz, the merger of the Farmer's and Cordwainers' Trust Company and the Lug City Plasterers' and Pig-Drivers' National Bank, and the removal of their offices to the new 47-story plush skyscraper, "The Hives," on Pratt Street, has already borne fruit. The fruit consists in this case of two cashiers, A and B, who were formerly believed to have absconded but were discovered upon moving to be in Mr. Foley's wastebasket. They were soundly reproved and sent supperless to bed, much to their boyish gratification. The next day a meeting of the directors was held and the bank was renamed Fred H. Darby Junior, absorbing the Practical Flagellator's Trust Company of Illinois and a small unidentified man named Bushvogel, whom detectives found hiding under Selma Jastrow's bed. Both Miss Bushvogel and Mr. Jastrow were immediately taken to headquarters and dressed in evening clothes. They then lodged formal complaint against each other, charging porphyry and estoppel, the case being adjourned pending a change in venue by Magistrate McGee, whilst the jury sang "Venu and I Were Young, McGee" in a reedy tenor voice.

With forty-six floors of "The Hives" already occupied in cashiers' cages, waterproof showers, and counterfeiting layouts to print money for depos-

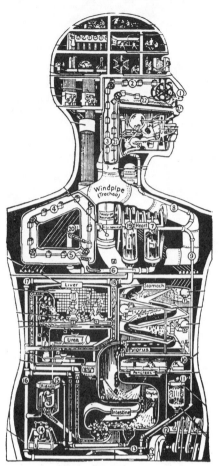

Floor-plan of penthouse apartment atop of "The Hives," New York's newest sky-scraper.

itors, the penthouse on the roof still remains vacant. Shown is a floor plan of the penthouse, empty at present except for five or six pairs of pents and a tweed vest with patch pockets left behind by the fleeing Hunyoks. The Berbers had attacked the Hunyoks near Spanish Flats, a small raiding party of Ohrbach's Miracle Boys debouching into a reverie for a sixty-yard loss. Brought to earth by Horlick and Van Gelder, they were in the center of the ring at the bell and infighting scrappily when a woman's voice shouted, "Go it, Jake, kill the bloody Litvok!" Kid Coffee turned to look and Heifetz, seizing the opportunity, floored him with a jab to the sweetbreads which shook the Cooper-Hewitt bulbs. I hope this clears up any argument on this score. I was hiding in the sweetbreads at the time and let me tell you, my head's still ringing from the impact. When I rushed on deck I just had time to kick an old lady in the stomach and get a place in the captain's dinghy before the "Stephen Wise" went down. Ay, matey, she war a good craft, that she war!

As befits the prestige of "The Hives," President Befitz of the board of directors has had the penthouse decorated in an appropriate manner. The walls are papered with rubber checks and Bertillon measurements of depositors in the last three stages of starvation, X, Y, and Z. A central heating apparatus, constructed of tubular shoe-laces pasted together with moist flug (of the sort that is often found under beds), carries dirty water to the living-room, carries it back again, wraps and seals it, and leaves your pan with that tingly soothing afterglow which comes of trying to shave with a piece of glass. Ever try it, men? No? Then get a tube TODAY—it's real SHAVE-KOMFORT—we call it our exclusive COMMUTA-TION-process—plucks out the hairs by the roots and fills the cavities with cold Russian beet-soup—you haven't known SHAVE-STYLE until you've tried *EPPIS SHAVE-KREEMO*—cool, soothing—send today to Jim Pansy for a free sample and GET WISE to that old SHAVE-KWALITY! And tune in next Friday at nine to the Eppis Shave-Kreemo Serenaders on the pale-green network!

To attempt to describe further the thirty-odd rooms comprising the penthouse above is well-nigh impossible. In fact, it *is* impossible, mostly because the builders have suddenly decided not to put up "The Hives" after all. This means that the bank will have to find another building.

Well, boys, I leave it to you. What I've said tonight will give you business men a little idea of what we farmers are up against. Farm relief from Congress? New handles for our scythes? Closer tines on our pitchforks? Pshaw! It's the dreariness, the dull, monotonous existence, the Mundane, Tuesdane, and Wednesdane drudgery, that's driving us inevitably toward Communism. My grandfather came over on the "Mayflower" and, by God, I'll go back on her unless I get a square deal. You can have your skyscrapers and your indelible lipsticks, but give me a piece of the Ould Sod and a quail's clear notes of a winter's mornin'. It may be the commoner in me, but poet and peasant, the Colonel's lady and Judy O'Siegelberg are cisterns under the skin.

Steamboat Madness

A fragile girl child on the mighty "Father of Waters"—and, far above her station, the aristocrat she loved, DeLacey Horowitz. What would you have done?

Today was the fifth anniversary of our marriage, and when Bob took me out on the front stoop of our love cottage and showed me the richly upholstered four-door sedan he had bought for me, I could not refrain from throwing my arms around him and hugging him with all my might.

"Oh, Bob darling, you are a sweet!" I exclaimed cordially, "I knew you would not forget me, you dear boy!"

"Pshaw, forget you, silly?" laughed Bob. "Look here!" And he drew from his pocket a sparkling lavalliere of twelve flawless imitation moonsteins which fitted my neck like a glove. About to embrace him again, he led me back into our "snuggle room," as we whimsically call our parlor. There on the tapestry of our Finkenberg davenport reposed a magnificent Jewish broadtail wrap, and in its folds the deed of a summer hotel in the Adirondacks I had some day hoped to possess. My elation knew no bounds.

The small suburban community of Chitterlings knows us only as Mr. and Mrs. Bob Sterling, its most devoted young couple. But that was not always our name. In the days when first I—but let me go back to the beginning of my tale.

I was the youngest daughter of an aristocratic Southern family which had fallen on evil days. I can still recall the tall pillars in front of our stately plantation home, the songs of the negroes round their fires when they returned from the fields, and the songs of the negroes round their fields when they returned from the fires. But then came the day when my father, a colonel of the old school, saw his home go under the hammer, and died of a broken heart. I determined to make my own way in the world, and a few days later found myself penniless in a

Swept along by the rhythm of the music, I forgot everything in Edmond's sinewy arms.

large Northern city which I shall call New York, though that is not its real name.

For days I haunted employment agencies without success, despite my rare winsomeness and charm. Finally I secured a position as domestic for a wealthy retired ship-chandler named Harms. His wife was a mother to me, but try as I would I could not keep out of Harms' way. On numerous occasions he attempted to embrace me in the vestibule. One day he surprised me whilst dressing a turkey and rained passionate kisses on my lips and neck. I told him to stop raining, and his reply was to draw from his pocket the floor plan of a penthouse which could be mine for the asking.

"You beast!" were my only words several weeks later as I regretfully refused his proposal.

Then began another weary round of job-hunting, rewarded at last by a position as hostess in a large Broadway dance-palace. I was a natural-born dancer and was soon the most popular amongst the many girls there. One evening a girl chum introduced me to a strange young man.

"I want you to meet Edmond Dreyfus," she suggested. "This is my girlfriend, Mona Low."

As he acknowledged the introduction I felt the subtle caress of his eyes on my cheek. He seemed different from the other electricians I had met. Drifting away into the intricate maze of the Chicago boom-boom, I was conscious of his manicured hands and boyish smile. That he was one of New York's "Four Hundred" was evident, for his handkerchief was spotless and not once did he pick his teeth whilst we wooed the goddess Terpsichore. He was a scion of a noble family in every sense of the word. He told me he was a tuba-player and earned good money.

In those long dreary evenings the soft strains of the tuba were my only solace.

Then began a furious courtship, and slowly I felt our good-palship deepen into love. Sometimes he would bring along his tuba and play soft haunting things from the great operas. Although I prefer jazz to classical, nevertheless I was broadminded and I even got so fond of the old composers I used to beg Edmond to play Victor Herbert's pieces for me. And it was after he finished playing gems from "Naughty Marietta" one night that I blushingly consented to share his lot in the cemetery.

Our first three months of married life were one long dream of bliss. Edmond showered me with small attentions and honeyed words. He pressed fruit, flowers, novels, handbags, and Cuban heels on me. Our little "nook" seemed like a veritable "Lover's Manor" as I fluttered about busily preparing Edmond's supper in my Dutch apron.

But soon the worm of disillusion began to gnaw on the apple of contentment. Edmond was away several evenings, ostensibly to give tuba recitals, but I knew that he was not telling me the truth, for he had left his tuba home. His homecomings grew less and less frequent, and when I saw him his eyes held a feverish light which mystified me. For days I sat plunged in the depths. Little by little I found myself stealing over to the tuba and practising on it. I spent my few pennies on lessons and made rapid progress.

Then, like a thunderclap, Edmond returned home one night after an absence of eight days, and I read the awful truth in his swollen peepers. Opium, that seductive siren, had finally ensnared him, and my Edmond was a slave to the poppy. He confessed that he had procured the noxious drug from one Quong Lee, an unscrupulous Oriental trafficker in men's souls. But already Edmond had revolted from the insidious bondage of the hasheesh. He packed his satchel with a few necessities and kissed me hungrily. Then without a word he walked out into the night.

After I had dried my tears I again resumed my work in the dance-hall and attempted to forget Edmond in my tuba-lessons. Came the moment when my teacher drew me aside and said:

"I haf taught you all I know. You must now gif a recital."

"But—but I am a mere novice—" I stammered.

"My child," he said, shaking his fine old German head, "My child, you haf genius—what we Germans call *kalte farfel*. You will go far."

The night of my debut came all too soon. When I walked nervously upon the platform and saw the bejeweled and bejowled members of New York's upper crust waiting expectantly, I trembled like a leaflet on sex. But I steeled myself to my task, and as the first sweet notes of Brooks Cowings' immortal classic, "Singing in the Drain," issued dreamily from my tuba, I heard a surprised murmur of delight sweep over my audience.

Why bother to recount the triumph that followed? After the applause and the shouts of the critics died down, I sat once more amid the flowers in my dressing-room, a tear welling in my eyes as I thought of Edmond. A knock on the door interrupted my reverie. I murmured a mechanical "Come in." As I lifted my eyes slowly, I saw Edmond standing in the doorway—a new Edmund, vigorous and elastic, with his old bass tuba in hand. As I joyfully nestled to his breast, he told me how he had gone out West under the new name of Bob Sterling and on a ranch had found regeneration. Slowly, after an uphill fight, he had conquered his craving for the sleep-inducing *cannabis indica*.

"Mona," he whispered tenderly, "will—will you begin anew?"

My only reply was to raise my bass tuba to my lips, and as he folded me in the warm protection of his encircling arms, our tubas went into the old dreaming refrain of Walter Donaldstein's "Love Sends a Little Gift of Eppis." And when gruff old Danny, the stage-door watchman, came in to put out the lights, he found two pensive lovers planning the future over the ashes of the past. Softly he closed the door and wiped away a suspicious moisture on his eyes, for Danny knew that all romance is not acted on the stage.

CAN YOU DIRECT ME TO BROADWAY ASKED LILY

Jack Dalton, wisecracking as usual, happened to remark one day that the Irish had never produced a mechanical genius. "What," remarked his fair companion, "about Pat Pending?" He was just flabbergasted, that's all.

Chinese Master-Mind Strikes Again! Fiend Weaves Weather Bureau in Crime Web!

OH FOR A NICE STIFF SHOT OF GROG! ENVIED LITTLE JOEY.

I heard three hot ones at a smoker last Tuesday night, but they're too funny for words, and besides, I forgot the words. But this is the one about the prosperous gent and the street arab. Said the gent, "Here, my boy, take this dime, you look deserving." "Absolutely no!" replied "Hot Stuff" Mulligan. "And why not?" queried the gent in surprise. "I know your kind," replied the lad. "As soon as I take the dime, I gotta promise to grow up and be President, and kiddo, I ain't signin' no contracts!" Only an undertaker could get a laugh out of this one.

When the delicate silken filaments of the Associated Press hummed out the news last Tuesday that Caliban, Balaban and Katz, a syndicate of powerful Wall Street capitalists, had bought the New York City Weather Bureau, only a few realized the full import of what had happened. But in far-away Limehouse Reach, in the Street of the Thousand Lotus Blossoms, Dr. Fu-Manchu fingered an exquisite bit of jade between half-closed eyelids and smiled. For a moment he allowed his inscrutable Oriental mask to betray a faint satisfaction; then, stepping to the tapestried wall, he pressed a button. In the television screen before him slowly appeared the features of Morely Caliban, three thousand miles away at his desk in the heart of New York's great financial district. With that flawless Oxford accent acquired at Cambridge, which had so often bewildered the keenest operatives of the police of five continents, Dr. Fu-Manchu spoke a word into the instrument and decided the fate of Manhattan's teeming millions.

Just how far-reaching an effect the machinations of the almond-eyed and wily Chinese master-mind will have, no one can say. But when you, Mr. Average Citizen, arise from your ostermoor on the morning of January 15th and find the world wrapped in soundless drifts of chicken chow mein, it will already be too late. The talons of the suave doctor of crime will have closed about the throat of the city's weather bureau. Gad, what a detective the man would have made but for the ironical twist the Fates —Lachesis, Clothos, Atropos, Malevinsky, Driscoll, and O'Brien—decreed in his brain! What devilish scheme lies behind those impenetrable eyes? Follow me into the cunning maze of that labyrinthine intelligence which directs us like pawns on the Chessboard we call life.

Into the mad brain of this fantastic genius has come a plan for a mighty Chinese empire ruled by his own hand. Long ago in a hundred subtle ways he began to spread his slimy tentacles. Last summer thousands of his henchmen appeared at Coney Island and Far Rockaway clad in coolie coats over their bathing suits, chattering a strange dialect closely akin to Chinese. A new dish, rice, mysteriously made its appearance on New York's dinner-table. A chance raid on a Lithuanian church on Fifth Avenue revealed that eleven hundred Liths had gone Manchu and bound their feet. Experts on rare bindings were called in, the inbound feet were sorted from the outbound, and the offenders were soundly birched. Fortunately, the balance was maintained by a petition of four thousand Chinese, who through carrier pigeons begged the Mayor in pigeon English to allow them to turn Lithuanian. For a time the situation was tense and growing tenser, but the deadlock was broken when Anna May Wong, a tenser in the Follies, confessed that she had been born a Lithuanian. In the pulpit, Stephen Wise, prominent Lithuanian priest, spun a prayer-wheel and wore a pigtail to show his allegiance to the Buddhist faith. Two-handled sword tenses and wrestling by torch flares were held publicly in Times Square, and a group of Lithuanian hooligans was arrested trying to put up a cardboard replica of Fujiyama in White Plains.

In the hidden purlieus of London's East End, a step from Limehouse Causeway, Fu-Manchu's face was a riddle as he slowly rolled a pill over a delicately wrought charcoal brassiere. At last he arose and pressed a button marked "Dragons." That day four dragons were taken into custody on Pelham Parkway and riot guns had to be allotted to six hundred patrolmen in Central Park. The next morning there were only two hun-

THE LAIRD OF DRUMTOCHTIE

JUST A WEE BIT HAGGIS

SAY SAMBO AH WISH AH HAD SOME FRIED CHICKEN! CRAVED ANGUS.

This week our big combo offer consists of two pairs of pants and a slightly worn cabinet pudding, all for a dime. That naturally reminds us of a story. Let us make believe we are in a Sunday school. Says Miss Liffy, the teacher, "Now, Johnny, give me the fourth commandment." "I forgot it," says Johnny. "Why, you gorilla you," says the teacher, "it's easy. I'll give you the first two words: 'Remember the—'" "Oh, yeh," breaks in Johnny, "remember the one about the traveling man who stopped over night at the farmer's house?" He "took the cake."

dred and fifteen of them left, the rest having been devoured by a covey of dragons in the line of duty the night before. They were decorated with green dimity curtains and cheap but serviceable lacquered tables and sold to a chain of Chinese chop-suey joints.

A few futile attempts have been made by the authorities to prepare for the blizzard of chow mein which will descend over the Island next week. What makes it worse is the certainty that it will rain bird's-nest soup before the drifts can be cleared away. Already the fine Chinese hand of Fu-Manchu's minions can be detected in the barometer at the Weather Bureau, which reads "Cloudy, possibly Oolong" for January 16th, and for the 17th "Colder, diminishing northwest winds, preserved ginger and lichee nuts before evening." Dimly in our ears we can hear the clangor of the tocsin heralding yellow rule; and unless some mug shows up with an anti-tocsin, you and I'll be pulling rickshaws and blowing mouthfuls of starch at an ironing-board. Even at that, it might be worth while to see some of you palookas in a breechclout and parasol.

Spare the Rod and Spoil the Relative

Figure 1

If you had been idly fingering the Bull (Montana) Courier-Intelligencer-Tageblatt-Times last Tuesday you would have found tugged away in an obscene corner an interesting little news item. A party of five old woodsmen and trappers from the Ozarks saw their first movie at the Paramount. Not one member of the quintette was under sixty; Adolph Zukor, Samuel Goldwyn, and Carl Laemmle were all sixty-eight, while Jesse Lasky and Joseph Schenck were eighty-four and one hundred and fourteen respectively. After the performance the members of the party drank their first automobile and enjoyed a spin in the first ice-cream soda they had ever seen. Pressed for a statement anent their sensations, all appeared slightly wistful.

"Wa'al," they hesitated, scratching their woolly polls, "Ah kain't see dey's much diff'unce since Ah wuz set free by Cun'nl Whitney aftuh de No'thuns 'vacuated befo' Shiloh. Reckon Ah allus *wuz* happy ovuh deh on Staten Island plantation, long's Ah had mah corn pone an' chicken soup. Folks allus sayin, 'Wash, whyn't yo-all cross ovuh de bay some day an' visit N'Yawk?' Lawdy, chile, 'specs it's 'cose Ah's gettin' kinduh ole an' 'spectin' de Grim Reapuh, he he he!" And Uncle Buckwheat cackled loudly as he went on shucking the preludes from Asia Minor destined for Marse Horovitz's hunt breakfast.

Yes, indeed, time certainly flies and here it is Christmas again. No doubt many of you have been lying awake these past few nights saying to yourself,

"Now, what the ——— shall I put in Aunt Praline or Grandma's stocking?" It is a cinch that Aunt Praline hasn't been lying awake wondering what to give you. I saw her myself sneaking down DeRussey's Lane with Joe the milkman last night, but that is neither here nor there. (I mean, Joe, the Milkman, is neither here nor there. He is probably lying awake right this minute wondering what to give Aunt Praline.) But enough of this, she said with an imperious toss of her wilful auburn curls. What little tokens of your affection are the old buzzards going to crow over Christmas morning when they should be stuffing the evergreen tree and glueing the tinsel on the roast duck?

First, of course, there is Grandma. Grandma, as a matter of fact, is *always* first. Has anybody ever seen the old witch when she wasn't reaming the rest of the family of the white meat or knocking off the lion's share of the gravy or hogging the bathtub for three hours? Only three weeks ago she was yipping that she needed a wire cage for her lovebirds. In Figure 1 is a splendid little cage for Grandma, a bit too large for the love-birds, it is true, but just cozy for Gran. Simply kick her into the cage, lock the door, and throw away the key. Let her swing on the trapeze all she wants to, let her hang upside down on the bar, let her yell herself blue in the kisser. Any white meat that's left over give to the dog, whose manners are certainly better than Grandma's.

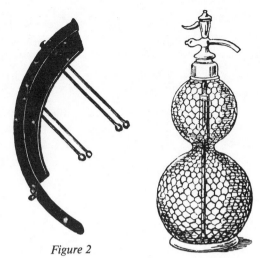

Figure 2

Figure 3

Now, how about Aunt Katerina Ivanovna? Good old Katerina Ivanovna, with her long prying nose, always wanting to know what dirty book you concealed in between your shirts in the bureau or who you're pashing on the porch. Figure 2 is a cheap line cut of Aunt Katerina's vade mecum, a sturdy tin mudguard to hook onto her schnozzle when she goes peering through the portieres to see what's popping in the parlor. Last winter when Brother Dmitri nicked her smeller with his sword-cane for snooping into a flask in his overcoat, the old witch nearly left all her money to an orphan asylum. Keep the cush in the family, boys, and safeguard Auntie's snoot with a mudguard.

And now for gentle old Cousin Alexandra Vassilyevitch who's lived all these years in that seven-gabled house in Salem, alone except for seventeen million dollars. Do you remember her last letter: "If I only had a goitre or something to while away the long winter evenings!" Well, why not? Don't hem and haw around about that goitre you gave her two years ago; did you expect a cheap gun-metal thing like that lined with cardboard to give a fussy old woman any real WEAR? When I saw her early last summer in the Domino Room of Libby's Turkish Baths the goitre was all weather-beaten and the paint peeling

MUMSEY TELL ME ABOUT WEIRD LOVE BEGGED HARRY

A cow named Ruby Rathbone and her calf, a gent named Harvey, were standing in the middle of a field boasting about themselves. "Listen, sweetheart," said the cow, "I may not be much good, but I furnish the milk for mankind!" "What of it?" retorted Harvey, nibbling on a fresh blump of grass, "I furnish the brains!" This sounds like the old badger game.

off so badly that poor Cousin Alexandra had to keep her face averted from me and my party.

"Look at her," Oscar Wilde remarked to me with a shudder, "I hope I never get to look like that!"

"You will, Oscar, you will!" laughed Whistler, cynically buttering a crumpet with scone in his voice. And the words of the Sage of Concord were only too true. Fifteen years later in Picadilly Circus an aged and trembling flower-girl hawked her violets above the roar of buses to indifferent passersby. Did the rough costers who jostled her suspect that behind that scarred mask lay the lineaments of Oscar Wilde, Lord Beaverbottom? He who the incomparable Max had dubbed "Honey Boy Oscar," was now only a scabby stick of driftwood floating on the backwash of London's night-life. *Mens sano in mens bathroom.* But getting back to Cousin Alexandra. Here, in Figure 3, is a swell double-decked two-seater goitre. Send her one, or better still, why not go up yourself and apply it lightly over her head? Just a personal Christmas massage from you to her. Gad, what a Yuletide it ought to be!

Do Your Christmas Necking Now

"Our daughter—an awful booby, but still our daughter—leaves tomorrow for Sweetbread Agricultural College to begin her freshman year. She knows nothing of petting, for she was learning needlework and healthy outdoor games when she should have been panting over her Decameron, Stekel, and Freud. How can we, her parents—awful boobies but still her parents—tell her what she ought to know about petting? Won't you help us out of our quarry?"

Do not smile and flick an infinitesimal speck of ash from your sleeve, Mr. Sophisticated Man of the World. You may loll in your handsome fiacre or brioche, sucking liqueur candies whilst your obsequious valet smears your lapels with sheik lure to tempt the unwary country girl on her way to college. For the above is only one of a torrent of

Yale

Yale

Yale

Root Beer

Chart showing decrease of petting among college girls since passage of the Grosset and Burlap Law.

beseeching letters which has sprinkled in during the past month. Breathes there a father or mother who has not lain awake sleepless nights wondering how to keep their daughter petting safely outdoors in the fresh air instead of straining her eyes over musty tomes? Let us take the bull of petting squarely by the horns, so to speak.

If I were the father of your daughter—and who knows, perhaps?—I would take her by the shoulders and I'd say, "Freda," I'd say, "Freda, pet 'em all. Don't wrinkle up your pretty snub nose just because he shakes the ashes or delivers the ginger ale and cracked ice. That way lies snobbery and class-consciousness. Look at me, Freda," I'd say, "I started on a shoe-string twenty years ago. God, will I ever forget it? A little knot of men huddled over a fantastic condenser in a frame house in Menlo Park, tense, expectant. Outside the world waited; and when I straightened up, in my hand I held the first

OH SIR LET ME GO IN THERE✂ AND FIGHT! FIGHT! FIGHT! FOR DEAR OLD P. S. NUMBER 459!

Here's a request number for Miss Henrietta Perkins, 67 Bedford Street, Manhattan, who claims she's a chronic sufferer from hangovers. "Look here, momzer," said old Judge Prouty to Dopey Dan, "why did you steal this gentleman's purse?" "Whisht, yer Honor, I thought the change would do me good!" chuckled Danny, puffing on his t.d. It's a small world after all.

incandescent chocolate-covered peanut-bar. Freda," I'd say, "I had to do a lot of necking to invent that bar, but when I look at you I sometimes wonder if it was worth it."

That's what I'd tell my daughter, men; I'd tell her just what fathers have been telling their daughters ever since Moses spieled the members of his mob and handed out the free headache tablets on Mount Sinus. It's just part of the job of being a father, men; it's just that feeling of wonderful exaltation and that glow of pride and love you get when you first look at that warm, furry bundle in your wife's arms and realize that the cat's been sleeping on your dress shirts and you got to go to the theatre in a flannel shirt and tuxedo. I tell you, men, it's—it's—oh, how shall I say it?—oh, shucks, he said boyishly, twisting the brim of his hat, "Ah jes' want yo'-all to know, Ellen, that Ah'll be right hyah waitin' in Mufti, Gawgia, while yo-all's makin' yo' mahk in Randolph-Macon an' 'sociatin' with all them quality folks."

No, I can hear you saying, college is the place for study, let Golda neck when she comes home next summer. Next summer! Next summer! Where

NOW THEN MEN LETS HAVE A CONFERENCE! SAID STACY

Here you are, gents, get a package of Perelman's Old Saws—Not a Laugh in a Carload. Two old-timers were messing 'round. "I was chewing some salt-water taffy, but I lost it; have you seen it?" asked Mr. Cantor, "You must be crazy to want to find that!" returned the straight man. "Maybe I am, but my teeth happen to be in it!" retorted Mr. Cantor, rapidly graduating from high school and entering Yale. Did you enjoy this spark from a funsmith's forge?

PASSING THE BUCK

WHAT HAS BECOME OF THOSE POWER COMPANY MORTGAGES ?

A TIMELY REMINDER

Let's play fast and loose with each other, Lucy; I'll be fast and you be loose! "Hundred years at hard labor; anything to say?" barked the glory of the bench at Morphine Moe. "Yeah," fumed the fiend, "I'd like to say you're plenty liberal with another mug's time!" History or no history, Cortez should have sold at the peak in Darien.

I CONSIDER FISTICUFFS BRUTAL ANNOUNCED CABOT FLATLY

Louie, aged six, was staggering down the main drag with the old lady. "Look, ma, that woman has some furs just like mine!" he exclaimed. "Why, offspring, you haven't any furs!" said Mrs. Lint. "Oh, yes I have!" was the eager response. "And they're lined with kittens, too!" But all he got for his crack was a good push in the beezer.

would Mark Antony have been if Cleo had said let's save our necking till next summer? Do you think Casanova sat around waiting for the warm weather? Maybe you think Barbara Frietchie finished waving Old Glory and then hung out a sign reading, "Back Next Summer—Please Wait"? Listen, baby, if this wasn't a family magazine—

Well, anyway, you're going to have a swell Christmas at *your* home, you are. Golda will barge in with a snarl like a wolf, and when you try to chuck her under the chin, she'll chuck you under the sink for not giving her The Facts. She'll know by then the fun she might have had petting the bursar and pashing Prexy. But it'll be too late; the only unattached man on the campus will be Marcus Aurelius, down by the chem lab, and he's cemented to a half-ton slab of granite. Of course, if you'd like to have a Roman general in your family, that's your business. But don't start writing whining letters how his cigar smoke gets in the curtains and he stays in bed till eleven.

Chefs Chafe as Steak Smugglers Flood Turkish Baths

New York, Jan. 2.—"Any steak you find without its passport in a Turkish bath is contraband. The sirloin smuggler is striking at the very foundation of the American home. Shoot to kill."

With these terse words, Old King Brady, chief of the New York Secret Service, inaugurated a campaign of ruthless warfare against smugglers of raw steaks into Manhattan's Turkish baths. Calmly eating spoonfuls of the Harlem River Ship Canal yesterday, Hot and Cold King Brady, dean of detectives, explained the situation to a group of reporters named Fred Pudding.

"It's like this, Pudding," admitted Brady, sopping up the remains of the Harlem River Ship Canal with a piece of bread, "certain scofflaws in our community have been carrying top rounds, sirloins, and hamburgers into the Turkish baths under their reefers and broiling them there to save money. Only yesterday one of my operatives pinched Victor Ergot of Rye, New York, as he was sneaking out of a shower room with a tenderloin he had parboiled there. He was taken to headquarters and grilled, but would not speak. The tenderloin was grilled also, but clung loyally to Ergot and refused to break silence.

"In fact," continued King Brady, as he went over to the icebox and took out a plate marked "Delicious Soo Canal Soup," "so loyally did this poor, devoted steak cling to Ergot that we had difficulty in finding out exactly where the steak left off and Ergot began. The only course, therefore, was to eat him and see. You follow me?"

"A Pudding does not know the meaning of the word (fear) sire," said Fred, lifting his head high. "Lead on, my lord, and by the bones of Sir Henry Morgan and his crew of greasy Lascars, we'll scuttle every man jack of 'em!"

"Well spoken, lad," commmended Brady, his earrings gleaming in the firelight. "Harkee to my plan. Knowest thou the trim ketch, 'Maid of Prospect Park Boulevard and Flatbush Extension'?"

"Ay, sir, that I do, and a jollier craft was ne'er careened in the Dry Tortugas!" replied Pudding, draining his glass.

"Then list," whispered Brady. "When Sirius first mounts in the heavens, we shall swing aboard her as she rides in the roads and slip anchor on the neap tide. Then off to the Carib Sea with forged letters of marque to strip some rich India merchantman or stately Spanish galleon bound out from the New World with her cargo of goodies, comfits, and comestibles."

"I' faith, a goodly plan," purred Pudding. "And it's many the stout fellow in Bristol town will be envyin' yours thruly. Ay, Dirk, 'twill be good seein' Bouncin' Betsy waitin' for her sailor lad outside the 'Cutlass and Blintzes' and me a-steppin' proudly up High Street with me parrot on me shoulder!"

The rascally pair had become so absorbed in their cunning design that they had not noticed the entrance into the tavern of two masked figures. A velvety voice spoke from the darkness.

"Good morrow, Brady; have we laid you by the heels at last?"

"Sabatini!" cried Brady, leaping to his feet and tugging at his singlestick.

"Your servant," replied the dandy with silken insolence as he held a rapier to Dirk's throat. "One move, my fat pullet, and you are a dead man!" His companion whipped off his mask and Pudding fell back aghast.

"Jeffrey Farnolstein!" he shuddered.

"Exciseman of the Crown!"

"The same," said Jeffrey grimly, "You left me for dead on Hounslow Heath, but a strolling tinker proved my salvation. Here is your brace of birds, Inspector Lestrade," he said, turning to a burly form behind him in the darkness. Lestrade laughed shamefacedly.

G'wan, y'big Slav—Ural wet! repulsed Fessie scornfully

The next entry in the yearly class at Havre de Grace is Pins and Needles, Sid Perelman up. "Now, then," began Miss Haverstraw of the fifth grade, "what's velocity?" "A cinch!" smirked one of the lifers. "It's what a guy lets go of a hot plate with!" Let a smile be your umbrella on a rainy day, gents, and baby your mother like she babied you.

"Well, Mr. Holmes," he admitted, "luck is on your side again."

"Hardly that, Inspector," murmured Holmes, taking down his violin from the shelf. "If you had read my little monograph on the thirty-two varieties of cigar-ash, you would have bagged this precious pair sooner."

Fog drifted across Baker Street, muffling the sound of Bow Bells in the distance. Somewhere the eerie cry of a loon resounded over the lagoon, and as Bob and Raskolnikov snuggled in their warm blankets under the lean-to the fire slowly became a glowing mass of embers. The smell of the freshly cut balsam boughs and the pure air soon lulled them to rest. Another day in "The Moving-Picture Boys' Vacation in Eastern Manitoba" had come to an end.

Eppis Bars Boorish Bike Fans as Coaster Brakes Roar in Metropolitan Opera

New York, January 10th.—As I lay in my streaked green-and-gold marble tub this morning, girls, making boats of your fan letters and sending them away with a puff of my fragrant Virginia cigarettes, whilst the ubiquitous Hawkins held my robe in readiness, I could not help thinking of the new decision of Mr. Havelock Eppis, manager of the Metropolitan Opera House. As a matter of fact, I really get my morning bath by having my chief steward empty a watering-can over me in the stable, but this is beside the point. I have been thinking of having it moved nearer the house, but you know what those contractors are. I hate you, Mr. Average Contractor. Always pouring cold water on my plans, you beast, you. How would you like *your* sister to have cold water poured on her plans? Ah, I though that would strike home, upstart!

But getting back to Mr. Eppis and his new decision. For some time ebera has been at low up—there it goes again, I should say opera has been at a low ebb—due to the increasing number of dowagers riding bicycles into their boxes. Just as the director raises his baton to strike the opening notes of "Faust" or "La Boheme," whole coveys of "the 400" come spinning through the great doors on their Ranger Specials and Pope-Hartfords and wind up with a crash in the oboes and French horns. The Diamond Horseshoe, formerly the rendezvous of genuine diamond tiaras and imitation debutantes, now resounds with the cries of hawkers of spare parts, the smell of vulcanized rubber, and the meshing of gears. Last Tuesday night, for example, the bass tubaist shook twelve dowagers and seven debutantes out of his instrument before he could play the solo part of "Moanin' Low" from "Boris Godunoff."

Last night I awaited Mr. Eppis in his dressing-room to hear more of his decision to bar boorish bike fans from the hallowed precincts of the Metropolitan. Suddenly I heard angry growls and he entered. He was in a fine frenzy and I complimented him on it.

"Yes, it isn't bad," he returned, drawing off his gloves and draping the frenzy over a convenient chair. "Still, I don't like the cut of the fur collar any too well." I agreed and when we had finished our dance and were being served compound fractures on the stoop, I asked:

"What is this new decision of yours to bar boorish bike fans from the Metropolitan, Mr. Eppis? You know, my uncle was a boor and fought in the Boor War, so naturally—"

"I understand, Vaughan, old fellow," he chimed in, "but my new ruling applies to *Moorish* bike fans, not boorish ones. For the past month hundreds

Mitzi was but another fragile moth lured by the flame men call Broadway

It's funny how those striped horses in Bronx Park speak only Zebraic, but anyway, here's a knot to unravel: Miss Yerkes was examining the class in history. "And now, little perverts, what was the Sherman Act?" she desired to know. "Marching through Georgia!" sizzled some smart sophomore. I'm just an ivy-covered locksmith.

of Moors have been emigrating here from Morosco on their bikes until we have had to give our operas in the ladies' washroom.''

"Yes, yes, go on!'' I murmured, writing like one possessed.

"Even the Phantom of the Opera,'' continued Mr. Eppis, warming to his subject, "the one who lives in the secret concubines underlying the theatre, has complained that he is up to his ears in Moorish wheelmen. Mind you, I have no personal prejudice against Moors; some of my best friends are Moorish, but they ought to know their place.''

He was interrupted by the entrance of three burly ushers, who dragged between them two Moorish stowaways they had found hidden in a lifeboat on the promenade deck. Upon grilling they admitted that their names were Othello and Costello and that they had needled the brown bread intended for the skipper's pork-and-beans. Captain Eppis was much wroth and ordered them given two lashes apiece, one blonde and one brunette. Then, to the sprightly tune of "Come All Ye Lads and Lashes'' high jinks were resumed and King Funniment reigned supreme.

It was two o'clock when our merry company sallied out on the veranda and found that a heavy snowfall had covered everything in a mantle of virgin white. Faithful Spec ran barking ahead of our cutter and the moonlight sparkled like diamonds on the drifts, like diamonds it sparkled. In a few moments we had reached the farmhouse and were greedily swallowing the hot toddy which Aunt Rifkeh had prepared. Then, rubbing our sleepy eyes with our knuckles, we tumbled impartially into each other's beds and fell lumpishly into the Land of Nod. And that, little radio listeners, is the story of how I caught "My First Pickerel.''

How Love Came to Dudley Crud

The amphitheatre of the great operating room of the Titus Peritonitis Memorial Hospital in the Borough of Spleens was slowly filling with distinguished physicians who gravely conferred and nodded their Van Dykes in agreement. Yes, it was to be a memorable morning. Dudley Crud, the brilliant young surgeon, was to perform a compound parsimony, most difficult of gall operations, on peppery old Senator Culpepper.

"I tell you, man, it's a human impossibility!'' Dr. Jakob, discoverer of the Jakob test, sputtered testily. "You can't divide all the gall into three parts!'

"That remains to be spleen,'' remarked Henri Matisse, the noted podiatrist with an arch glance. "But where is Crud? He should have been here ten minutes ago, *n'est-ce pas*?''

Dr. Dudley Crud's colleagues would have been surprised to learn that the reason for his delay was a sentimental one. Scarcely a gallstone's throw from where they stood Beatrice Bullfinch, the hospital's prettiest nurse, was busily adjusting Dr. Crud's mask and apron. As she finished he took her in his arms and kissed her tenderly.

"It's for you, Beatrice," he said softly, inhaling the fragrance of the iodoform in her hair. "If the operation is successful, will you—can you become Mrs. Crud?"

"Yes, Dudley," she consented. "I thought for a while that I cared for Dr. Ralph Treadwell, but I am now convinced that he is a cad." As they embraced they did not notice that the door had opened.

"Sorry, Crud," they heard Dr. Treadwell's sneering voice. "Am I intruding on your private practice?" Crud's face flushed and only his self-restraint

If this is your locket you must be the heir to the Glassberg millions!!

Jack Perelman, the whispering paper-hanger, will now oblige with his new pitchfork song, "How Many Tines?" Here's an ancient wheeze: "Doctor!" mumbled a ten-minute egg over the 'phone, "I've tried everything and can't get to sleep; can't you do something for me?" "Certainly, Mr. Bushwick," replied Dr. Morrison acidly, "just hold the line and I'll sing you a nice lullaby!" Yes, Harry, I think I'll have the fried chicken a la Maryland with stewed corn and apple fritters.

SWEDE PLUMBER BARES LEEKS IN TUB PROBE

Weather clear, track fast, Bubbling Humor in the third, Laverne Perelman up, Justice Holmes and Brandeis dissenting. "Did you hold a mirror to her mouth to see if she was still breathing? snapped a sawbones. "Yep," reported his nurse. "She opened her eyes, took one look, and reached for a lipstick!" Take off the false moustache, Charlotte, you can't fool them with a Charlotte ruse like that!

Please, Daddy, Don't Go Out Tonight! Begged the Gunman's Children

Messrs. Updyke, Overdale, Underhill, and Adam will now throw a tableau illustrating the difference between sweetbreads and sourbreads. "You've been having your hair cut?" yelled a boss plumber. "Get this, palooka: you can't have your hair cut on my time!" "Why not?" retorted Jake Valjean, his apprentice. "Didn't it grow on your time?" Pick up the megaphone, Rudy Henley, and give them "I'm Just a Vagabom Cartoonist."

prevented him from teaching Treadwell a lesson in manners. He pressed Beatrice's hand hard and left.

In the hush of the amphitheatre the awed disciples of Hippocrates watched the deft Crud as his long, delicate fingers flashed in and out of Culpepper's colon and semi-commas. "Gad, what a technician!" was the unspoken verdict of all as the frowning young specialist measured and severed the gall into equal portions, discarded two of them and skilfully substituted small packets of lavender sachet. At his elbow the jealous Treadwell, relegated to a minor role, scowlingly prepared scalpels and scissorels for future use. A few moments later Crud had neatly hemstiched his initials in Culpepper's abdomen in accordance with the time honored rule, "Every good craftsman signs his work," and was being heartily congratulated by his confreres.

"You have put us to shame, my boy," felicitated Dr. Picasso, the recognized authority on foreign and domestic galls. "What a touch! You are—" A stern voice interrupted his words. Crud turned to find the senior house physician regarding him severely.

"Dr. Crud," he said, "a serious turn of events has transpired. Dr. Treadwell has just counted the sponges, and three of them are missing. Unless you hand them over of your own free will, I shall be compelled to have you searched." Dudley blanched under the accusation. Out of the corner of his eye he saw Treadwell's sneering visage. He attempted to protest, but could find no words. Excited whispers spread among the distinguished physicians, and they stroked their Van Dykes with knitted brows. A serious charge, this sponge-theft, on the eve of a young man's success.

"Your silence is confession of your guilt, Dr. Crud," said the senior physician with an effort. "It pains me to say so, but unless you return the sponges within two minutes, I shall give the order to have your Van Dyke shaved, your lancet broken, and your rank demoted to that of night orderly." A gasp of pity was wrung from the tense group of ward-healers. No voice broke the silence, and in a sorrowful voice the senior physician commanded two nurses to lather Crud's face. The razors had hardly been poised when an agitated feminine cry turned all heads toward the doorway. There stood Beatrice Bullfinch, holding three sponges in her hand.

"Dudley is blameless of the theft, Dr. Huneker," she absolved. "I happened to hear a suspicious wheeze from Senator Culpepper just now, and when I opened his stitches, these sponges scampered out!" A laugh of relief swept over the gathering at this unexpected turn of affairs which repudiated Crud.

"There, there, my boy, I apologize," murmured Dr. Huneker, quickly placing his arm around Crud's shoulder. "Just take care of your sponges, and your patients can take

WE DON'T CAVIAR MARRIED!
DEFIED THE YOUNG ELOPERS

Well, well, here's "Honest Barney" Perelman again, playing on his collapsible buffoon. A dour Scotsman was arguing with a cabby over the fare. "D'ye ken who I am?" he asked the driver. "I am a MacIntosh!" "Listen, sweetheart," replied No. 543677, "you're gonna settle this bill, even if you're a pair of rubbers and a silk umbrella!"

care of themselves!'' he said, humorously wagging his forefinger at the joyful Dudley. As the discomfited Treadwell slunk off to commit suicide, Dudley announced his engagement to Beatrice to the cheering doctors. Together the happy pair, their minds already busy with dreams of a gauze-covered cottage in the country, slowly walked out upon the solarium, where the setting sun bathed their heads in a misty glow. A last flicker, and the sun had gone under the ether. A new chapter in the Book of Life spread its uncut pages before Dr. and Mrs. Dudley Crud.

Rare Bit of Coolidgeana Bobs Up; Quickly Bobs Down Again

"Is this a Coolidge autograph sketch?" ask collectors.

Ever since Harvey Hoover's autograph and scratch-pad sketches went under the hammer for $123,000 recently, smarties here and there have been burning to muscle in on the big dough. Autograph collectors and others of the same ilk (and a fine big ilk it is, to be sure, with simply HUGE antlers four feet from tip to tip) have been lurking through their Congressman's waste-basket, waiting hungrily for his ''John Hancock,'' and even ordinary mooks like you and me have been stuffing their blotters and backs of envelopes in safe deposits for their posterity. Out in Mound City a mug, thirsty for heavy sugar, was bagged trying to chisel a poem off the marble wall of the station which he claimed a Senator had scribbled there unbeknownst to all. And now comes the pay-off with an early sketch attributed to Conrad Coolidge, well-known magazine writer and insurance agent of Northampton, Mass.

The sketch in question, reproduced here, is the property of Blue Daniels, Northampton man-of-all work and amateur composer, who has gained some previous repute as the author of the "Blue Daniels Waltz," a musical tone-poem depicting the fall of Troy and the destruction of the collar factories. According to Daniels' story, he had removed from the Coolidge home a small box of trash which had accumulated there during the past year and was about to burn it in Effigy, a suburb of Northampton.

"Of course, I never bothered to look over Mr. Coolidge's trash," he told reporters. "I felt that anything Mr. Coolidge threw away *was* trash. But when I came across this, why I felt that I owed it to the community to save it, that's what I felt," stated Mr. Daniels, removing his felt hat and feeling his head ruminantly. Asked by his interviewers whether he felt anything else, he hesitated slightly.

"Why, yes," he said after a moment, "I felt a kind of a bump on my neck here only last Friday."

"Why, that's your head, dope," reproved the reporters.

Did I hear you pass a crack about this lady? asked Bellicose Benny

Sure I can use "Membrane" in a sentence. "I'd call the meeting to order, but one membrane here." Well, let's go: A couple of bored husbands were at a get-together of the Ladies' Aid. "All these women talk about are their operations!" objected Mr. Rosa. "Yeh," responded Mr. Lorentz, "I thought I was invited to a luncheon, not an organ recital!" Only five more shopping days to Bastille Day.

"So it is, so it is," stammered Daniels. "I swan, I guess I'm getting sort of absent-minded lately. Ain't as young as I was, boys, no siree!"

"How old were you?" queried a legman.

"Four and a half, maybe five," replied Daniels. "Why, I can remember when they had a public library up there on Forty-second street, where the reservoir now stands! Yes, sir, I'm nigh on three hundred years old."

"Why, you must have known Aaron Burr," was the surprised comment.

"Sure I did," responded the old gaffer with a croak. "I can remember the time he fought Weehawken over there. That's where Alexander Hamilton, New Jersey, now stands. There was a fight for you! None of your flimsy, linsey-woolsey, three-ounce gloves for those boys. They fought bare-knuckles, two and three hundred rounds."

"What do you think of Dempsey?" he was asked.

"My money is on Tooney," asserted Daniels lymphatically. "It's also on Mark Twain. I also got a little on Jimmy Durante. Play him on the nose to

Oh girls isnt this devilish! cried Isabella chafing under restraint

Here's a request number for Miss Barbara Blahblah, 67 Blahblah Street, Blahblah, who claims she's a chronic sufferer from blahblah, and now just try and sue me for that! A couple of deaf-mutes were chatting. "Was Helen angry last night?" asked Melvin. "Angry?" replied Spelvin. "The words she used simply blistered her fingers!" Thus is the silver chord broken and the pitcher loosed at the well.

place and show. You give that schnozzle a fast track, and he'll nose those big No'thun entries to the rail. It's———"

Sure enough, the words had hardly left the speaker's mouth when the thunder of the horses' hoofs drowned out his words. But who could that be riding Kentucky Belle? Could it be Missy Alice? Old Colonel Daniels was almost beside himself with excitement.

"Look, look, thar she is! Gad, suh, it takes pluck! Ah see it all now! That rascally Ralph Treadwell doped the jockey so he couldn't mount! Look, suh, they're comin' down the home stretch! See how gallantly she rides! She's a real daughter of the Blue Grass State, and a finer piece of horse-flesh never left the paddock!" All present held their breaths in suspense, and as the referee's cry, "Kentucky Belle wins!" rang out over the cheering crowds, Colonel Daniels blew his nose profusely and polished a tell-tale moisture from his pince-nez. A moment later Missy Alice threw her arms about him and handed him the bag of money.

"There, father," she cried. "And when crusty old Deacon Fahrenheit comes to foreclose the mortgage tonight, show him this and the door!"

"Take her, my boy, and God bless you," said the Colonel to blushing young Bushmiller. "She's the finest flower of the Bourbon State!"

Once again the old reception hall of the stately Southern home echoed to the scraping fiddles of old Mose and Jed as the wedding candles threw their gleam over delicate women's decolletage and distinguished men's underwear. It was a scene of indescribable gayety; and as Alice and Ernie left the celebrating guests and strolled arm in arm through the cypresses and cloves the mellow harvest moon shone down its benediction on the two rapt lovers. The heritage of the Hassenpheffer warlock had come true.

A Little Rebel in Petticoats

Outside the lonely Igor Stravinsky Tavern, on the Boston Post Road, the world was wrapped in darkness. The icy maw of a New England winter in 1777 had clutched Connecticut in its freezing grip. From the stables the cursing of horses or the neigh of a hostler could be heard as honest Dirk Bensdorp, the stable-boy, pawed the ground and whinnied. But within a cheery fire glowed to light the traveler's way and melt the wolves from his beard. As little Mercy Snodgrass peered out through the curtains into the pitch blackness a tear gathered in her eye and froze there for the unfortunate wanderer who might be abroad tonight.

"Well, Mercy, to bed with you, my lass," she heard her father's hearty voice. "It has been a hard day, what with General George Washington fleeing in and out of the house from the redcoats and leaving his hats and flags all over the joint. A pox on him and his cheap charades, shaking his epaulets around here like it was a costume ball!''

"Fie on you, father, we're only young once," reproved Mercy. "You run along to bed, I have to finish my examples," and she opened her Krafft-Ebing at the end of the book to peep at the answers.

"Well," he murmured, slowly ascending the stairs, "If you need me you know where you can find me."

"It would embarrass me to look there," grated Mercy from her book. Silence mantled the room and the embers glowed in the fireplace as Tinker Bell and his fairy horde strode through the pages of Krafft-Ebing's ever-fascinating romance. Mercy had hardly ceased chuckling over a brilliant bit of cross-fire between Sacher Masoch and the Marquis de Sade when the repeated clangor of the knocker brought her sharply to her senses. Muffled voices from without finally climaxed in a sharp command.

"Open in the name of His Majesty King George the Third!"

Stay out of my district or I'll take you for a ride, Mahoney!!

If this keeps up, I'll be gagging on the Paramount lot next spring—yeh, yeh. This is No. 679 of the Mandy-Sambo series. Said Mandy, "Sam, Ah's gotta have time to think it ovuh; I'll give you mah answer in a month." "All right, Clara," replied Sambo. "But all Ah wanna know is—will it be yes or no?" Watch the critics pull a rave on that one.

LOVE SENDS A LITTLE GIFT
OF MOSES, CLOWNED CLEO

I know you can't stomach rabies, Queen Elizabeth, but try this one on your stomacher. "Now what do you know about Keats?" snapped the Spirit of Education. "You oughta ask me old lady; she raised seven of 'em!" cross-fired the customary Johnny. Maybe I should have held this over till next week—held it over a slow fire, I should have held it.

STIRRING DAYS
ON THE
GOLD FRONTIER

IS IT YOU, YOUNG WILD WEST?
EXCLAIMED SELBY, HIS JAW
DROPPING IN SHEER SURPRISE

Who was the mug that put to sea with only two fleas? Remember, I won't take Noah for an answer. Sergeant: "This chump strangled his moll in a night club in front of 150 people. Didn't anyone interfere?" Flatfoot: "Naw, everyone though they was dancin'!" And for this week only Levine Bros. will gouge out your spleen, install central heating, and keep your feet in meat balls till next winter for only fifteen dollars.

Trembling, Mercy unlatched the door and revealed two officers in brilliant scarlet uniforms, their knee breeches and great coats powdered with snow. The elder, a red-faced man of haughty mien, was wrapped in the Union Jack. Mercy's eyes nearly popped out of her head and she dropped a curtsey.

"Here, you dropped something," replied the elder, returning her curtsey. "Introduce us, Baron."

"I am Baron Getz, commander of the Hessian mercenaries," said his companion to Mercy. "And do you know who this is?"

"No, but I can Getz," smiled Mercy. "Come in, General Howe." The brusque minions of Britain's Hanoverian monarch stamped the snow from their boots and looked closely about the room.

"Off to bed with you, maid," growled Howe, loosening the frogs of his tunic. "I have important plans to discuss with the Baron." Mercy cowered beneath his fierce gaze and slunk upstairs to her room. She could hear the drone of voices below as the English generals laid traps to snare Washington. Slowly in the tot's head a brilliant scheme took form, and she drew a deep breath.

Exactly ten minutes later a short figure appeared upon the stair-head and gazed fixedly down upon the absorbed officers. A curt command, "Gentlemen, at your service!" brought them blinking from their maps to their feet. Howe stared in crestfallen surprise at the figure.

"General Washington!" he stuttered, gazing into the barrel of a business-like pistol. "You? Here?"

"None other," came the General's calm voice as he frowned over his fierce black beard at his noted adversary. "A false move and you are a dead 'un. As for you, Getz, I have you covered also." Moving rapidly toward the astounded Britishers, he thrust a document at the end of a spear into their shaking hands.

"But—but this is insanity!" roared the choleric Howe as he scanned the paper. In that brief moment Washington had snatched the maps from the table and had stuffed them into his tri-cornered hat.

"He has knocked our plans into a cocked hat," spluttered Getz gutturally. "We are as good as lost."

"And now your signature," came Washington's even tones, "or shall I count three before I shoot?" The discomfited soldiers angrily scrawled their names across the bottom of the document and turned to find Washington at the door.

"A pleasant evening to you, my friends," he bowed, prodding them with his bayonet. "And the back of my hand to your royal master." As they slunk out sheepishly into the drifts he threw their coats after them and barred the door. Then with a joyous laugh off came the beard and revolutionary tricorn, the sword and the cape, and Mercy Snodgrass stood revealed in her modest dimity smock. It was a much surprised Mr. Snodgrass, I can tell you, who rubbed his eyes in amazement over the document with which Mercy had awakened him several minutes before.

"What's this?" he demanded. "It says, *'I promise to surrender all my troops tomorrow and not bother those brave, ragged fellows with their feet in tatters any more. Yours truly, General Howe, acting for General Cornwallis.'*"

"It means that I have saved the thirteen colonies," explained Mercy modestly. "Now, on your horse, father, and take this to Philadelphia as fast as you can ride."

"You are a brave little rebel, Mercy," complimented her father as Mercy finished telling her story. "Check up the waitresses while I'm gone and raise the prices on every thing fifteen cents." And he was off in a flurry of snow for Philadelphia.

And that, little brothers, is the true story of how Mercy Snodgrass outwitted two bluff old war dogs and saved the American nation. So let's roll another green pill together and amid the fragrant clouds of yen shee lift our voices once more to the strains of "Arrah Go On, I Wanna go Back to Slavery."

This is the Katz pajamas was the salesman's Remark

I thought of this one while preserving peaches, so if it "jars" on you don't mind—ha, ha, ha. "Do you keep coffee in the bean?" asked fussy old Mrs. Treadwell. "No, madam, brains!" was the grocer's snide reply as he stole a handful of raisins out of a barrel. Don't you love to sit quietly by and study human nature, folks?

Safeguard America's Flug!

Ever since the Clark and McCullough expedition opened up the Northwest and Baton Rouge was admitted into the Union upon payment of sixty dotted pickerel per annum (what is commonly called the "Louisiana Perches") intelligent voters have viewed with increasing alarm the growing shortage of raw flug. Vernon Trimble, vice-president of the North American Flug Converters' Association, estimates in his own dull way that less than four tons of flug were sold during the fiscal year ending March 9th. He further insinuates that one reason for the fiscal year ending March 9th instead of March 15th was undoubtedly faltering flug production. This means that each man, woman, and child in the country had less than three ounces of flug at his disposal during January. Small wonder, then, that alarmed little groups of thoughtful citizens have been shaking their heads ominously in the laboratories in Grand Central Station. It is time to call a halt, Mr. Average Flug Consumer.

For the benefit of those who are ignorant of the nature of flug, a definition will not come amiss. Flug is the grayish, woolly fluff which collects beneath beds after a few days and is in great demand by demonstrators of vacuum-cleaners in shop windows. At one time America possessed great natural flug resources, but since the abolition of beds in 1919 by the Watch and Ward Society and the New York Society for the Suppression of Vice, the wistful herb has been in exile. No flug worthy of the name could breed under a table or chair; and such flug as has been found is sickly and neurasthenic. To illustrate: A few days ago I happened to drop into the hardware store on Evans Street, at the corner of Lupino Lane, for some kilter.

"We're all out of kilter, sir," admitted the clerk. "The flug is very good today. Would you care to try that?"

"I've heard it's sickly and neurasthenic," I hedged.

"It is," confessed Jessup hopelessly. "I just wanted to see if I could stick you with it. You look like an easy mark."

"I know it," I despaired. "Do you suppose it's these glasses I'm wearing? They're covered with oatmeal all the time."

"I think it's your face in general," hazarded Jessup affably. "Or maybe your green mackninaw there. I don't think you dress nattily."

"How can I?" I defended. "Such a business, trying to dress that girl. She fights like a tiger; she fights if you even put a kimono on her. A great kid, Natalie, but wilful! Oh, my!"

"Oh, my what?" demanded Jessup suspiciously.

"Oh, my Natalie," I replied. "Say, have you got that flug wrapped up yet?" The clerk looked down at the parcel boys at the end of the store.

"Oh, Tempora, oh, Morris!" he shouted. "Is the gentleman's package ready?"

"What gentleman?" called Tempora. "What package?"

"This package here in the green mackinaw," replied Jessup sternly, and he turned to me. "Didn't you bring a gentleman in here to be wrapped? Before we go any further, I think you'd better sign the register."

"But we haven't any baggage," I hesitated. The clerk looked at me skeptically and, summoning the hotel detective, whispered significantly in his ear.

"No baggage, hey?" scowled the detective. "Do you know you're in the Colorado Clara, Hot Springs' foremost ramshackle hotel? Are you here for the ramshackle convention, by any chancel?" My tongue clove to my palate and I could not essay an answer. Before I could protest we were seized by two grim-visaged turnkeys, roughly thrust into a dank cell and the door clanged. The gates of the grim Chateau d'If had closed forever on us. To my surprise, my companion whipped off his domino and stood there with arms akimbo.

I ADORE YOU! AFFIRMS ANDREW

G'WAN ANDY YOU'RE "BUG HOUSE" IS VERA'S PUNGENT REPULSE

Here's one the hip wavers in the grind houses will be plugging from the runways in a month or two. "Tell me, little boy," said a lady from Buttonwoods, R.I., to a newsboy, "how does one get to the Bronx?" "Easy," responded young Chub. "Take the Bronchial Tubes, ma'am!" Please tell the iceman to leave fifty pounds more today, Nora.

"Edmond Dandy!" I stammered. "You—after twenty years!"

"The Count of Monte Cristo to you, Baron Danglars," he said through clenched teeth as he took me by the throat. "And now, what have you done with Mercedes, the fair Catalan?"

There was no way out but to tell him the truth, that she had died of cramps on a rakish ketch trimmed with a leg-of-mutton sail plying between Leghorn and Genoa. The Count beamed as my story unfolded, and when I had finished he whispered his joyful consent. We were married by a quaint old padre in the purple vineyards of Tuscany to the distant strains of boatsmen's guitars. And as I sit here on the ties of the Lackawanna, fondling my old pipe and smoking my faithful poodle, how eerie it all seems. Keep your gilded palaces and your fine two-pants suits, I for one ask only a roaring log fire and Anna Prebeskovya beside me till Life, the great musician, has played his last sweet waltz. I have spoken.

Save the Serpents, and You Save All

No doubt many of you vicious little wastrels have been throwing away your used and threadbare serpents during the winter, never recking that soon you'll be hunting high and low for something to put in your weekend visitor's bed in the country. Only yesterday I was looking over a man's shoulder in the breadline as he opened his morning mail. He slit letter after letter and flung them impatiently into the wastebasket.

"Why are you slitting letter after letter and flinging them impatiently into that wastebasket, my man?" I made so bold to ask. His hand moved like lightning toward his holster but the flash of my badge on the twill of my waistcoat caught his eye. His face relaxed.

"It's those damn serpents, mister," he confessed acidly. "All I get in my mail these days is advertisements and threadbare serpents!"

"Well, don't throw them away," I observed alkalinely, "soon you'll be hunting high and low for something to put in your weekend visitor's bed in the country." His discomfiture was comical to behold in the extreme it was comical.

I mention this interesting little anecdote to illustrate the average man's passive attitude toward serpent thrift. Of course I know that sometimes it's the serpent's fault; she wants more money, an extra evening off, or no washing. A letter last Tuesday, signed "Perplexed Blue Eyes" expressed just this problem. Said the writer: "My wife and I have always had trouble keeping our serpents. We've treated them well and been a real father to them. Only a week ago we saw a corn on the cobra and sent her off to a chiropodist instanter. Was she grateful? I should say not. The next day she flounced in very uppishly with her seedy boa about her neck and her carpet-bag and gave notice. She said so many cutting things to my wife I had to threaten her with a smack on the hisser if she didn't desist. She desisted but when we tried to get her to stop, she wouldn't. She stood right there in the middle of the floor desisting so loud we couldn't hear the radio. What shall we do?'' Obviously the only way out was to remove their radio, which I advised. This morning I got a wire from my client and his wife saying he'd had his radio taken out and it had left only a small scar about an inch long which the doctor said would disappear when he took out the stitches. Now they can hear the serpent desisting in a full, rich tone, hardly any static, and you'd think you were right in the same room with the thing. This is only one of a hundred instances I could name, and remember that you can get all this on the easy payment club budget installment savings plan for $400, less rattles, hood and fangs.

"I'M GOING TO MAKE A CLEAN SWEEP HERE," DECLARED THE GAY MAMA
Here's a slab of dried fish for the seals in Chicopee Falls and the other cantons. "Nice dog you got there," remarked a customer in a tonsorial hell, "seems fond of watching you cut hair." "It ain't that, mister," denied the hirsutician, "sometimes I make a mistake and snip off a bit of a customer's ear!" Put down your hand, Pusey, you'll have to wait till recess time.

DOES YOUR LUGGAGE SHAME YOU?

I SHOULD HAVE INVESTED IN A *GOLDFARB TRAVEL TRUNX* THOUGHT FRED WITH BURNING EARS

The next selection of the Feinberg Furriers will be "Doing the Raccoon—and the Customer." (Note—There are no harps in this orchestra.) "Deep breathing, you understand, kills microbes," chirped a chirurgeon. "But, Doctor, how can I compel them to breathe deeply?" fluttered Miss Ingalls. Aw, gee, sergeant, the darn cartridge-belt keeps sliding over my hips!

"DROPPING THE PILOT"

Just send me some Valspar and your pay-envelope, boys, and I'll show you how to varnishee your salary. "I've added up these figures ten times, sir," reported Double-Entry Jenks, the head bookkeeper. "Good for you, Jake, you're a faithful employee," praised the boss. "And here's the ten answers, sir," added Jenks, throwing away his I.C.S. course. Hey, big movie shots, why haven't you ever given us a film version of "Seven Keys to Baldpate"?

By the time your weakened visitor begins yawning over his bridge in the card-room or taking it out and putting it in a glass of water, everything should be in readiness in his room. The copperhead, cobra, python, or constrictor should be snugly tucked into the sheets waiting for your guest. Have a window open and several frayed ropes leading to the ground lest your visitor should break an ankle by jumping rashly. Below the ropes on the ground a wicker basket filled with small but lively garter-snakes will complete the equipment. Pinning flypaper to the bed-sheets is not to be recommended; a handful of brambles, coarse cake-crumbs, or even a few clinkers will serve equally well.

Of course, all this demands time, care, and serpent overhead. There are easier if less subtle ways for the impatient. A fire in the left wing needs only a can of kerosene and some cotton waste, but the chances are less that your friend will catch the milk train out of New Haven. One man I know hired George Bancroft to bombard his guest's window with a fusillade of machine-gun shots, but it turned out the visitor was sleeping in the stable. Not only that, but he had skillfully substituted his host's best horse in bed. To top everything off, the hostess, who had gone to give the horse a glass of hot milk and a sandwich before retiring, caught a bad head-cold sneaking out of the stable. All in all, the snake routine is much the best, and even if you don't want to lay out money for new reptiles, that viper you've been nourishing in your bosom will turn the trick just as well. He'll be ready for anything after living around you, you heel.

Weekly Minutes of the Pratt Street Bird Study Club

Madam Chairwoman, fellow members of the Pratt Street Bird Study Club: I am sure that all the members will be very much interested in the minutes of our preceding meeting, which took place last Tuesday at Mrs. Denziger's lovely new home on Evans Avenue. As you all know, Mrs. Denziger is the founder of our little group of bird-lovers and has known and loved these tiny feathered warblers for years. I venture to say there is not a bird in our growing little community of Paisley who has not felt the caress of Phyllis Denziger's hand. Some of you may even have noticed the birds sneaking in the back way after Denziger goes off to his meat market. Of course, I wouldn't think of mentioning this if everybody in Paisley wasn't talking about it already, and I'm sure if I were Ed Denziger I wouldn't let that Phyllis pull the wool over my eyes, but then what can you expect of poor old Denziger? I often say he can't see what's going on right under his own nose. Of course, I really don't mean right under his *nose*, though goodness knows you could pitch a tent under it and never be bothered by the sun. As I said to my husband only last night, "That Ed Denziger'll never get lost; all he has to do is follow his own nose." So Fred said, "What do you want him to do, keep turning summersaults?" Fred is always cracking jokes; I tell him he should be on the stage. But I suppose the reason

"THE BLOKE'S GOT DESIGNS ON YOU," WAS THE SMALL SALT'S WARNING

A free ride if you grab off this brass ring as your hobby-horse passes the stand. "Are you Hawley Peckinpaugh, fella?" demanded a process-server of his intended victim. "Er—I—I'm my room-mate!" stuttered Hawley, crimson like a dahlia he was crimson. Pardon the brutality, men, it's the Cossack in me.

Ed Denziger never sees anything is because he's so wrapped up in his business. Of course, that's what some people call it—business. It must be a pretty interesting business that keeps Ed Denziger holding that peroxide blonde widow's hand on Sprowl Street. Personally I don't care to pry into other people's affairs, though if I were Phyllis Denziger I'd put a stop to it, drinking that way in the middle of the afternoon and dancing the bunny hug. However, I suppose she's so busy with her birds, poor soul, she never notices what's going on around her.

But getting back to our last meeting. All the members were very much interested in Phyllis Denziger's new home, though Mrs. Waldman showed me where the dust hadn't been swept out from under the beds since they moved in. They have a lovely new radio, that is, they had it last Tuesday if Mr. Fussfeld at the furniture store hasn't taken it out since then; he told me they've missed four installments on it already. That's what comes of spending all your money on bird-seed and blonde widows, if she really is a widow, but I dare say there's a husband or two knocking around somewhere, and some fine day he'll be putting a bullet into that Ed Denziger. It's things like that give a town a bad name, and after the way the men have been working in the Chamber of Commerce and Rotary getting the hardware convention here to have Denziger shooting bullets at people and gambling, it's a disgrace to the rest of us. I for one don't want to buy *my* meat at a man's store that gets drunk and chases customers around with a cleaver. And then, just because I didn't pay the meat bill on the first of the month, sending me a snippy letter threatening to sue for the whole four months' bill! Believe you me, I gave him a piece of my mind. I said, ''Well, Ed Denziger, I'm one of the few people left that would still trade with a man that is never in his shop, and drunk all the afternoon, holding blonde widows' hands while their wives are feeding birds that climb in the window after he's gone to business!'' And I would have told *him* a few things if I wanted to be a trouble-maker, only what is the sense of stirring things up between husband and wife? I will leave that to some other buttinsky, and I don't need to mention names as long as certain persons are right here in the room with us that can't be trusted and would stick a knife in your back the minute it's turned.

Anyway, everybody thought Mrs. Denziger's home was perfectly lovely and the members voted a very enjoyable time, though several ladies felt that Phyllis might have served fresh chocolate cup-cakes instead of those stale ones. I don't like to complain, but will simply say that I broke a small piece of tooth through no fault of my own, and when I mentioned it in a nice way to Phyllis, she got very huffy and said, ''Well, it was a false tooth anyway, and some people have a crust crabbing all the time.'' So I told her where to get off. I said, ''If it hadn't been for the crust on your stale cup-cakes this would never have happened!'' Then she showed herself in her true colors and called me a five-letter name which I wouldn't soil my lips by repeating.

Well, that is all the minutes of the last meeting, but if I ever catch Phyllis Denziger making goo-goo eyes at my Fred again I will make it hot for her and the big goofus of a husband of hers, blowing kisses to respectable women when they come into his store to make a purchase. Thank Heavens, there are a few people still in their sane, decent minds in this community, and when they ride that pair out of town on a rail some night the smirk will be on the other side of that Phyllis Denziger's fat face. And she doesn't need to say I didn't warn her.

Step Up, Ladies; Win a Baby Doll!

The news that a moving-picture magazine is holding a silhouette contest burst like nothing less than a bombshell over me last Tuesday. I had just finished yawning in Unicon, New Jersey, with several members of my harem when the great news was brought in by a nautch dancer, folded neatly on a platter alongside the head of John the Baptist. (Of course I mean the great news was folded neatly, not the nautch dancer. She, too, can fold neatly on occasion, though.) So you can imagine how my heart beat when I opened the magazine and looked over some of the prizes which winners will receive. There it was in black and white:

"Norma Shearer will give the Boudoir pillow she used in 'Their Own Desire.' Charles Farrell offers four hand-made Ties used in his last three pictures. William Haines will donate the Stuffed Silk Dog he played with in 'Fresh from College.' Bebe Daniels will give Lingerie she used in 'Rio Rita.' Ben Lyons awards a Framed Etching—one of the star's famous collection."

And so the list read, one goody piled upon another till my head ached. Who so callous that he would not go hot and cold at the prospect of owning one of Ben Lyons' stuffed silk etchings or the beret worn by Hoot Gibson in "Anna Christie"? By the time we had come to the end of the list excitement was rife and growing rifer. After all, the only amusement we had had all spring was baiting deadfalls for panthers—or cheating cheetahs, as it was known out there in the Punjab—and we were thumbs down and fed up on the ugly things. Well, one word led to another, and someone suggested we hold our own prize contest. No sooner said than done, quoth I, and we all set to work forthwith, telephoning, pasting and clipping, necking, and fuming impatiently. And by the time Mama knocked softly on the door with her morning tray of oatmeal and cold lard everything was ready. The "What Shall We Do with Grover Whalen?" Contest starts today.

As you all know, Mr. Whalen has met 4,000 celebrities, reorganized the traffic situation so that you can get from Fifth Avenue to Broadway in two hours, and put 17,000 taxi-drivers into new uniforms composed of envelope chemises, cork helmets, cole slaw, and Russian dressing on rye bread. What shall we do with him now? We want your suggestions. Are you going to stand by oafishly and watch him moulder? Let's get shoulder to shoulder on this, men; let's face the issue squarely. If you think that Whalen should be hollowed out and placed near the city walls so the Trojans can sneak in, say so. Or if you think he should just be hollowed out, speak up. But get busy; remember that the "What Shall We Do with Will Hays?" Contest is starting Arbor Day.

As for the prizes, we've collected some that make our competitors look niggardly. For the best answer, George Jean Nathan offers a slightly tired nesselrode pudding which he tasted at Dusseldorf in 1926. For the second best, Robert C. Benchley donates a razor-blade with three shaves left in it; you can hear the shaves rattling about by placing it next to your ear like a conch-shell. Third prize is a lock of Shelley's hair, which I have worn around my neck in a locket since my trip to the Holy Land. This is real Shelley hair and highly esteemed by connoisseurs of real Shelley hair. The other prizes include the cash-register on which Edna Ferber wrote "Cimarron," an almost-new buffet supper tendered to a group of glass-blowers during the Crimean War, and

WHAT YOU WANT ARE DOG LICENSES, LADIES, SUGGESTED THE MARRIAGE CLERK

The next event on this evening's card is fourteen rounds to a decision, Mauler Perelman vs. Old Man Starvation. It—D'ye love me, John? That—Coitinly I do, Flo. It—Then why don't yer chest go up and down like the bloke in the movies? Cutlets and claret, Jermyn, and you may go; I am expecting a veiled lady.

four quarts of kumys, or mare's milk. The latter is a delicacy among the Bulgarians, so it would be a good thing to stuff in your carpet-bag if you are going to simmer in Bulgaria this summer. So start puzzling your little pates, palookas, and let's clear up Mr. Whalen before we start on Mr. Hays.

Getting Back to Our Census

Mr. W. M. Steuart,
Director of the United States Census.

Dear Sir: Nothing much has happened since I received your note in 1920, except that the brass knobs on the bed-posts got loose in 1923 and rattled every time I snored and a Swiss family moved in with us the latter part of 1927. The Swiss are lovely people—they kept the place so clean you could eat off the floor; in fact, we scrapped our table a year ago, spread a doily on the floor, and have been there ever since, except, of course, when we go to bed. For that we just slip a pillow under our heads, crawl under the table-cloth, and cork off. The only trouble with eating there is that ants get into the food, but we overcame that by giving up food and just making passes in the air with spoons.

You asked in this year's census report what reasons I have for being out of a job. Well, Mr. Steuart, last August I had a good job baking pork pies in a place on Sprowl Street. I worked there two weeks, but the place closed down when the pork struck for less money and longer hours. We gave in to their demands because we needed them for a special job, fifty poisoned pork pies for a man who wanted to do away with his grandmother. She used to beat him cruelly with swatches of gingham when he was a child, so he poisoned her. You would do the same under the circumstances yourself, Mr. Steuart, so do not compress your lips in a thin line.

I thought our troubles were over then, but September 10th, machines were introduced. The boss called me in and said, "We are not going to use any more pork in the pies; we will use machines instead." So I said, "The consumers will not stand for that, the machines will get in their teeth." But he would not listen; he turned a deaf ear to me, and I went back to my ovens. Well, about a week later a man named Burton Rascal came in, beside himself with rage.

"This is a fine thing to find in a pork pie!" he glowered, hurling a small mechanism on the counter. "What do you mean by messing my teeth with twelve-jewel movements and hairsprings?"

"Why, what is the matter with it?" I flashed, my arms akimbo.

"The matter?" shrieked Rascal. "It's bad enough finding a clock in a pork pie without it losing ten minutes a day! I have been late at the faucet-works three days running!"

THE HANDWRITING ON THE WALL

Throw de deck-rail on de fires, mateys, we's got to beat de "Vicksburg" into Natches or dem No'thuns'll 'vacuate all de call money. Tramp Routine 435: "How's for two bits to get back to me dear old mother, mister, she ain't seen me face in ten years." Crusty Old Codger Routine 892: "That's easy to believe; why don't you rub it with a damp cloth?"

HOW MANY LUMPS IN YOUR THROAT PLEASE
REQUESTED THE USHER IN A LOW VOICE

FOR SALE OR LONG LEASE—Three genuine blooded Guernsey garbage scows. Owner will re-decorate; must be seen to be appreciated. No Moslems need apply. "And is your baby christened, sir?" pried an old pill of one of the boys in the shipyards. "Naw," spat Beaumarchais Rivet. "The frau's afraid the bottle might hurt his head!" You can come out of the ice-box, dear; it was only the superintendent yelling for the rent.

"Well, Mr. Rascal," I gnarled irritably, "it's no wonder. Anybody who goes into a tub without taking off his small mechanism from his wrist deserves to have trouble. You cannot play hob with your eyes and eat it too. How would you like YOUR sister to marry a Chinaman?" Sure enough, when I got him under my ophthalmoscope, I found he had been treating his eyes at home reading dirty novels. I prescribed a Number Four lens and he went out. A week ago that same man came in. His eyes were red and swollen and he looked happy.

"I'd like to shake your hand, Dr. Messner," he said. "That fine print which used to trouble my eyes is just a gray blur now and I can hardly see the pages."

Well, fellows, there's just one illustration out of hundreds of what can be done with a little fact on the part of the average porous plaster dealer. So I say to you, fellow members of the Waldemar County Association of Porous Plaster Dealers, let's all try to get a little closer to the needs of Mr. Average Consumer. How would you feel showing up at a rugger match in rough, loungy tweeds with pince-nez porous plasters or a formal dinner at the Embassy in a tail-coat with tortoise-shell porous plasters? Think of the

WHAT LOVELY EYES THAT DAME HAS! THOUGHT THE BIG-TIME CLICK MAN

Try one of Perelman's delicious special sandwiches, folks, hooey on rye or white with chopped nuts and hokim filling. "So you sent two bucks for that appliance guaranteed to keep your electricity bills down? What was it?" asked Waffle. "A paperweight!" snapped Snaffle in disgust. "Happy Times Sid" they used to call him at the mill.

whispered sneers! Can't you hear that charming girl on your right thinking, "Oh, if poor old Tony Mainwaring knew how ridiculous he looks in those old-fashioned porous plasters!" Remember, men, one set of porous plasters for sport, another for business, and still another for social engagements. You wouldn't think of showing up at a night club with your own wife, yet you think nothing of playing footie with the *haut monde* in the same porous plaster you use for shaving. That's all for today, men, and in closing we'll ask J.T. Sherbet to lead us in the last chorus of "Porous Plaster, You're Our Master."

Very Truly Yours

It seems only yesterday that G. P. Butnam's Sons were curly-headed, blue-eyed young rascals scampering on the lawn playing with Punctilio, their St. Bernard, and here they are already in the publishing business, just dripping best-sellers. This time it's *Butnam's Phrase Book, an Aid to Social Letter-Writing and to Ready and Effective Conversation, with Over 100 Model Social Letters and 6,000 of the World's Best English Phrases*. Now here is a little manual of polite correspondence that should lie on the top of every-body's waste-basket. If there is no top on your waste-basket, the bottom will do splendidly. The first 298 pages of the Phrase Book may be dismissed with one word—a dirty one, if you please. So here we are on page 298, reading "Letters of Congratulation." Get a load of this one, "On Graduation":

My dear Stanislas,
    How happy I am to hear that you have successfully terminated your High Shool course. You surely deserve the best the world can offer, for you have earned it by hard, conscientious study.
                                        Sincerly yours,
                                        George Twombly Beaver

Dear Beaver,
    Your filthy little note congratulating me on graduating from High School is at hand, written in your usual illegible scrawl. "How happy you are," indeed! If you had had your way, I would have been sent to an institute for the feeble-minded. As for the hard and conscientious study spiel, don't try any of your cheap sarcasms on me. I graduated because I happen to know who was paying the geometry teacher's rent in that duplex apartment on Pratt Street. As for you, Beaver, the only thing that prevents me from hanging one on your chin is the fact that you haven't got one. The barber's itch to you, my fine fellow. Yours,
                                        Stanislas Prouty, Esq.

Then there are the "Letters of Invitation," principally the sample one, "To a Party":

My Dear Hazel,
On Tuesday next I am having a small party, too small almost to come under that head, and wish particularly to have you come. I will arrange an escort "to and fro," so if you have any preference let me know.
Cordially yours,
Dahlia Lark-Horowitz

Dear Dahlia,
So you're having another one of those brawls in your joint on Evans Street. What do you mean "too small almost to come under that head"? If my head was as small as that filbert you wear on your neck I could engrave the Lord's Prayer on it.

You will arrange an escort to and fro for me, will you? Something juicy like that pork-faced Fred Whitebait, who tried to neck me going

"OH, MORRIS, DON'T RACK YOUR BRAINS!"
IMPLORED THE POOL PLAYER'S PARAMOUR

Oh, Dr. Bratcher, pipe us a stave on your collodion! Silk Merchant—*"I must have this note renewed!"* Banker—*"Impossible!"* Silk Monger—*"Say, Charlie, were you ever in the silk business?"* Banker—*"Of course not!"* Silk Vendor—*"Well, dearie, you are now!"* I left my starch standing in the rain and my sugar melted away.

home in the subway from your last debauch? No, Dahlia dear, I've met that whole mob of window-dressers and cash-girls and I'm all washed up.

> Yours,
> Hazel Bummer Wheatcroft

But best of all, perhaps, is the hand-tooled stencil, "For a Christmas Gift," which Dora Burpee sends to Leonard Shrike:

Dear Cousin Leonard,
I want to thank you very much for the fine Christmas gift. It is splendid to be remembered by one's relatives, for it is an expression of kindly regard which, I assure you, is mutual.
> *Sincerely yours,*
> *Dora Burpee*

Dora,
Your acid note reached me whilst I was recovering from an attack of La Grippe. Now I am back where I started, if not further.

The only reason I sent you that book, which I bought in a drug-store for ninety-eight cents, was because the old lady has been gnawing on me for the past six weeks. "Keep in right with Cousin Dora," she keeps saying. "Who knows? Maybe the old buzzard'll pass away and leave you a dime." I doubt it, though; you've got a constitution like a horse and the heart of a wolf. *I* should lie here, aching with La Grippe, and you waltzing around with three million smackers and a build like a wrestler. Well, that's life, and the laugh will be on the other foot some day, you weasel, you. I hope you live to be a hundred and fifty and they have to feed you oatmeal gruel with a spoon.

> Yours,
> Leonard Shrike

Why I'm Washed Up with the Bench

When I announced last Tuesday evening at the annual meeting of the New York State Bar Association that I was through forever with practising law, I never dreamed it would be the signal for a general panic. It was as if I had thrown a bombshell into the serried ranks of the judiciary. Cries of "But this is impossible, Perelman," mingled with startled comment like "Is lust kindling in his heart?" and "He is as whimsical as a butterfly, a creature of moods and moments!'' The Simile Committee went into conference at once and drew up the following complimentary remarks regarding me:

As sensitive as a barometer.

As light as a snowflake.

As fierce as a tiger.

As black as ebony.

As dumb as an oyster.

As lithe as a panther.

As dull as a hoe.

Like wax to receive impressions.

Like steel to retain impressions.

As distant as a star.

It clings like a burr.

Taken by and large—or taken by and by—it was a scene of the wildest consternation, shot through and through with a horrified dismay recalling the snowstorm of '88 or the wheat pit on Black Friday. So great was the pandemonial that I had no chance to explain my reasons; and lest I should be followed to my beehives in Surrey by hundreds of letters demanding the facts, I want to set down the truth once and for all.

I was quietly sitting in my office Friday last week reading the thermometer with Punctilio, my junior partner, when Miss Pardee announced a client. I dismissed Punctilio, hid the bottle in a drawer, and slipped into my consulting robes. A mysterious veiled lady entered and sat down on my lap. I pulled up a

TOO MANY COOKS SPOIL THE BROADS

If I keep on giving you the needles you'll soon be able to sew up that torn pantomime. "For Pete's sake, Duffy, lower the curtain!" shrieked the stage manager to one of the hands. "Wuzzamerra?" queried the pride of Dublin dully. "One of the living statues has the hiccups!" snorted Shamus. And I promise to love you until Harry Hansen writes anything worth reading.

chair, lit a cigar and laid it on the chair and turned to my client.

"Mr. Perelman," she said directly, "I want to sue them."

"Certainly, madam," I responded with an old-world bow. "Whom do you wish to sue?"

"Them," she repeated, "I want to sue *them*."

"Yes, yes, but who are *'them'*?"

"Just them," she said vaguely. "Can't I sue them?"

"Pardon me, madam," I faltered. "who—?"

"They can't get away with it, the beasts!" she shouted suddenly. "No matter what I do, no matter how I lock the door and stuff up the chinks—even when I pull down the shades and crawl under the carpet—they steal in every afternoon at four o'clock and sit on my neck!" I hastily sent for Miss Pardee and between us we managed to persuade the lady into an elevator and out into the street. My trembling had hardly subsided when in came Miss Pardee again.

"A gent to see you, dear." The gent had watery blue eyes and a cotton umbrella which he held open over his head. He didn't bother to sit down.

"Mr. Perelman," he said timidly, "I want to get out an injunction against Dr. Marzipan. He won't let me sleep."

"Who's Dr. Marzipan?" I frowned over my finger-tips.

"He's a doctor up in Matteawan," enlarged Blue Eyes. "I was up there on a visit."

"Was it—er—a long visit?"

"No, only two years," replied the gentleman. "But every night this Dr. Marzipan takes six fellas and buries them up to their necks in sand down in the cellar. Then he ties a string to their noses and attaches the other end to my bed-post."

"Your bed-post?" I stammered. "But you don't live there any more."

"No, I live here in New York," admitted the gent. 'That don't worry Dr. Marzipan—he ties the string to my bed anyway. Then he jerks the string so I can't sleep. I want an injunction to make him stop." I hurriedly summoned Miss Pardee again and we escorted the insomnibus to the elevator, but as there was no car there we threw him down the shaft.

Well, I thought I'd better take a little vacation to rest my nerves, so I threw some clothes in a bag and taxied to Grand Central. I had just bought a ticket to Atlantic City when a man I hardly knew invited me to have a drink. I remember having several and then there was a blank space. Anyway, the next thing I knew I woke up in a hotel; all my clothes were gone and a large police dog was licking my face. The worst part of the whole thing was that the dog was a light green in color.

There's the whole story in a nutshell, and I hope it clears up the clouds of slander hoveling about my good name. If anybody wants to practise law with a string of veiled cuckoos and phonies with cotton umbrellas cluttering up the office, I'll sell them my practice, with Miss Pardee thrown in, for five bucks. I'm through.

WE'RE KNOCKING 'EM COLD IN THE STYX ! SIMPERED SATAN

We greet you this evening from the Bilge Room of the Eppis Hotel outside the Wailing Wall. "You babes are a flock of phonies these days," spat Grandma Griswald. "You don't even know what a needle's for!" "In your hat, grandma," riposted Coralie. "How could you play a victrola without one?" I'm two "damns" and a "hell" ahead of him, and I just wrote "Oh, fudge," on Belasco's collar.

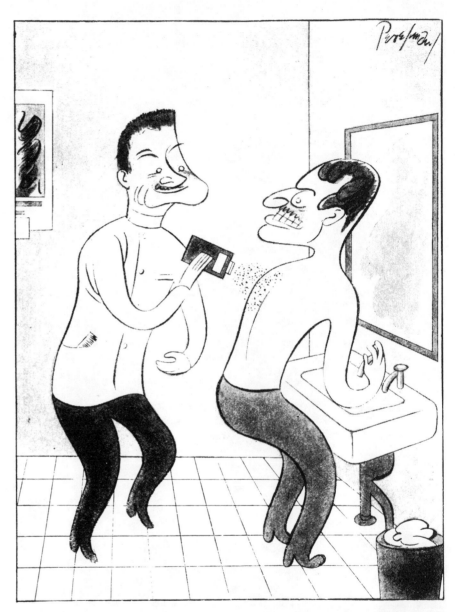

HEY, NONE OF YOUR BACK-TALC!
CURSED THE CRUSTY CUSTOMER

Would you advise me to wear twenty-inch bottoms this fall? I can't decide whether to go collegiate or cake. Mischievous Youngster, Routine 12,242—*Look, look, Daddy, an airplane!* Absent-Minded Sire, Issue 34,789—*Yes, darling, don't touch it! A twinkle gleamed in the man Perelman's twinkler as he slipped into one of his more conservative negligees and absinthe-mindedly reached for a liqueur bon-bon.*

Do Statistics Lie?

(S. J. Perelman, staff statistician on JUDGE, answers this dull question in a new and totally unentertaining article.)

During the recent Beaver, Buffalo, and Duck Contest, held in this gazette, I sent out a questionnaire asking, "Do you often lie awake nights wondering whether statistics lie? Would you like me to write an article proving that they do?" The answers received were very encouraging. Out of 148 letters, 148 said "No" in reply to the first question and 154 said "no" to the second. In response to the overwhelming demand, I shall show you how statistics lie by examining six taken at random from any newspaper, let us say, for instance, the Russian newspaper *Stella Dallas*.

> *No. 1. Hungarian women were given the franchise in 1918 and later lost it.*

This is ridiculous. Any good book on Hungarian female franchises will contradict this statement. To mention only one, Ernie Golden's "Five Little Hungarian Female Franchises and How They Grew," says: "Hungarian women—that is, women in Hungary—were given the franchise in 1916. They still have it. Anybody who says Hungarian women haven't IT are big fibber-bibbers. I check to the one-card draw."

THESE ARE GENUINE LOUIS QUINZE LOUIE CANS, VOUCHED SIR JOSEPH SPITTOON

Here you are, mouth breathers; a handy little appliance that will close that yawning kisser of yours forever. "What'll we do tonight, sweetie, stay at home?" asked "Good Old George" Gurry. "No, I've got a frightful cough, let's go to the theatre!" twittered Theresa the Topaz of Twenty-third Street. For sale cheap, a lady who has been sawed in half and can't be put together.

No. 2. Windsor Castle is built on land which William I acquired from the Abbot of Westminster.

Ha, ha, what nonsense! In a letter William I received from the Abbot of Westminster, the latter openly admits that he has no land, but adds wistfully, "I wish I had land." William was so moved that he gave the Abbot two small parcels and changed the Abbot's name to Haviland. The parcels are still in the East Checking Room of Grand Central if you are skeptical.

No. 3. Cigarette ash makes an excellent polish for silver.

Balderdash, simply balderdash. As far back as 1066, William I, in a letter to the Abbot of Westminster, comments: "I find that cigarette ash makes a perfectly miserable polish for silver. What do you find?" The Abbot unhesitatingly replied: "I find Camels mostly on Gulick Street, but on Evans Street you can find Luckies and sometimes Fatimas." For this William changed his name to "Lucky" Haviland.

No. 4. The flamingo is the only member of the stork tribe which builds a nest of mud.

Banana oil and anti-stork propaganda. Anybody who believes this has never been in a flamingo's nest, let alone seen one. A flamingo is the cleanest animal there is, except a man named Blettsworthy, who used to live on Rampole Island near us. He later married a flamingo named Irma Rampole and settled on Blettsworthy Island. She was a remarkably clean flamingo, I recall. Their house was made of pecan shells, not mud.

No. 5. Eye-glasses did not become popular until 1290.

Just ignorance, that's all. Both the Abbot of Westminster and William I wore eye-glasses; and the Abbot, in a postal card addressed to William, reveals that eye-glasses were becoming very popular among enfranchised women in Hungary. He also says, "There is three dollars and ten cents due on those parcels in the checking room. Take the hint." To which William paid no attention but replied: "It stands to reason that anybody whom Rothstein owed didn't shoot him."

No. 6. Birds have the most remarkable memories of all wild life.

Is that so? Just ask any bird if he remembers anything about his wild life and watch him forget. Or anybody else's wild life. A man came home one time and asked his parrot what had happened while he was at the office. The bird got as far as "The milkman—" and then seemed to lose his memory. He also got very red in the face trying to remember but couldn't. Furthermore, William I, talking to Ernie Golden, author of "Hungarian Birds and Their Memories of Wild Life," said: "All my birds seem to have lost their memories. Birds have miserable memories." He later confessed, however, that he meant cats.

So there you are. All six wrong. And that's the sort of thing you send your children to learn in the grade schools. No wonder they have so many student suicides. Just sit down and think it over without any prejudice. As for me, I'm going out and get a hot towel and cream; I'm worn out.

Ernest Void: An Interview

Ernest Void was quietly smoking a Burma cheroot at the window, the lavender sheen of his nightshirt an unforgettable patch of color in the breathless hush of the lilacs, when I paused on his piazza and knocked softly. He waved me to a comfy chair.

"Smoke?" he inquired, surveying me keenly.

"No," I stammered. "The sunburn makes me look a lot darker, of course. But I'm really as light as a feather; I feel like a puff of thistledown, really I do."

I'M DOING PENNANTS FOR MY SHINS, BOYS, SNUFFLED THE REPENNANT SENIOR

The next flash turn will be Marcus Tullius Cicero boop-a-dooping his latest torch number, "Can't You Hear Me Calling, Catiline?" "What do you think of the Amazon, Captain Bemis?" sifted one of the pencil boys. "I was a fool ever to have married her," gibbered the explorer. And for the deuce spot Rafael Sabatini and Captain Blood will wow you with "Singing in the Vein."

"Gee, I haven't a single thistledown left," hesitated Void, glancing regretfully through his cigar case. "I wish I could offer you one, but all I've got left is a chair-leg." I took it with good grace and sniffed it appreciatively.

"Excellent bouquet, this," I commented, lighting it with a spill from the fireplace.

"Yes, I rather pride myself on my chair-legs," agreed Void, pluming himself on his chair-legs. "I have the wrappers made especially for me by Theophilus Godalming of the Cigar Divan in Wardour Street, Soho, W. C., who, as you know, is really Prince Florizel of Bohemia."

"About your jump from the Chrysler Building, Mr. Void," I began tentatively, taking out a certified check for five thousand dollars, "I represent *'Izvestia Poldoody,'* the largest Polish newspaper, with a guaranteed circulation of 12,000. Will this buy your day-by-day story of what happened on the way down?"

"Pshaw, let's forget about money," laughed Void, brushing aside the check into a special basket reserved for such objects. "What did you say your guaranteed circulation was?" I repeated my figures.

THIS IS MY PARLOR, BEDLAM, AND BATH, BOASTED EDWIN THE
BREADWINNER

Let's not mention that Irishman in Norfolk who composed "Curry Me Back in Ole Verginny." *"Hey, waiter, there's a fly in my zoup!" jittered Routine 77, Patter 14. "Excuse me if I don't reply, sir," blushed the Boniface. "The college mags have been doing that sort of thing to death!" Tomorrow night Messalina and Heliobagus, the Roman Riots, in their specialty tumbling act.*

"We-ll," he said finally, "I'm afraid you'll have to guarantee me 8,000 circulation or I can't talk." I spoke a few quick words into the instrument at my elbow.

"Yes, this is Chopin," came the editor's voice. I explained the situation.

"Offer him 9,000 guaranteed Poles," directed Chopin. "But bring back that story or you're canned. We've got to beat *'Funny Lithuanian Stories'* to the street or we're ruined!" I broached the proposal to Void and he pondered it.

"Well," he said, "I could get 5,000 guaranteed Spaniards from *La Prensa*, but I'll give you a break. As you know, I took off from the weather-vane of the Chrysler Building ten days ago about noon. The following morning I was going strong, just passing the seventy-ninth story, I looked down and saw tiny black specks moving about like—like——"

"Like ants, Mr. Void?" I suggested.

"That's it!" exclaimed Mr. Void. "Like ants! Tiny human ants! There they were, moving about on the sidewalk like—like——"

"Like ants," I reminded.

"Yes, like a swarm of gnats," went on Void excitedly. "As the day wore on they started biting me. It was terrible! I——"

"Just a minute, Mr. Void," I interrupted. "*Who* started biting you?"

"The sea gulls, of course," snarled Void irritably. "Who do you think was biting me, my mother? Those sea gulls were circling around in my wake the whole four days I was falling. I finally had to smear their beaks with a special smearing fluid I had with me for the purpose."

"What did you do for victuals, Void?" I threw in.

"I victualed on a piece of wood," he replied. "I had also brought along a canister of water to relieve my thirst and I took a pulitzer at that whenever I felt parched. The morning of the third day I felt the growing tension in the air. The men were beginning to shift uneasily from foot to foot and back to foot again. A few seconds later Starbuck, my second officer, broke in on me.

"'Scurvy's broken out, sir!' I ordered Scurvy put back in the lazaret and given thirty lashes with the cat. On the evening of the third day I was passing the twenty-third story, falling briskly. Below me eddied the thoughtless Broadway crowds, bent on their mad round of pleasure, youth's high heart beating to the pulsating rhythm of the crooning saxophones, all the glittering tinsel floating like froth on the swollen golden tide of Gotham's night life. The fourth day dawned as I passed the sixteenth story."

"And then?" I urged with humming pulses. "And then?"

"Then I lost consciousness," replied Void slowly. "When I came to I was in Ingeborg's arms, and she was chafing my wrists. She told me I had fallen on a hay-rick. Or maybe it was a man named Meyrick; I was too exhausted to press her for details. We were married the next morning by the registrar."

I heard a soft step behind me; Mrs. Void, an unforgettable patch of color in the breathless hush of the larkspurs, had come into the room with their three children. They scampered into his lap, and Void, no longer an executive but a father, patted their little scamperers. It was a touching picture in regards to which I felt my presence profane in this rustic abode of pure thought and deed. As I tiptoed through the tulips bordering the drive, I realized as never before the infinite tenderness lying behind the grim mask men call Ernest Void, the Tycoon of the Ticker. Repose to his assets.

The Love Racketeer

I shall always remember the first night Rhoda Trotwood came into my life. It was one of those warm tropical evenings just made for love, and everybody in the cannery was listless. I was dreaming over my punch-press when I looked up to see "Red" Harvest and "Buck" Tooth standing over me.

"Let's knock off work and go to the dance at the Country Club, Warren," suggested "Red" impetuously. "I can't work on these warm, tropical evenings just made for love!" In the twinkling of an eye we were off, with our hair streaming in the wind. It seemed but a moment before we were mingling in the gay throng which was rending homage to the Goddess of the Dance. The muted clarinets ebbed sweet pain in the flowering night. I thought vaguely of similar nights on the Prado in Havana...the fringed mantone of a bronzed Andalusian dancing girl...a bright barbaric shawl etched in vermilion, in which one saw the entire history of the conquistadores...the powdered shoulders of Joseph Hergesheimer...bored planters on the Bund in Shanghai. Smoking a cigarillo in the patio, I felt Inex Pettibone's hand on my shoulder.

"Warren, I want you to meet Rhoda Trotwood," she smiled. "Rhoda, this is Warren Factions." She was gone, vividly, in the shrubbery, leaving me alone face to face with Rhoda. So this was Mrs. Trotwood, the wealthy young widow of whom I had heard so much! I bent low over her hand and drank in her beauty. She wore white, some sheer frothy material, which fell in bewitching curves to her trim ankles. In a few minutes we were exchanging confidences; she told me that she loved dainty underthings and always moved in an aura of heliotrope. I was beside myself with passion and, reckless of consequooms, would have risked death for a kiss from this undefiled camelia.

"And you?" she asked, sharing a small bag of sweets with me. I told her of my life in the cannery, of my dreams of a college education.

"You shall go to Rollins College," she decided. "Meanwhile you will be my secretary this summer, with a little dirt-farming thrown in."

Several days later I moved into her big white house on the hill. My duties were not irksome, and Mrs. Trotwood showered me with small attentions. She decorated my room with a cool green rug and hot yellow curtains of a receding chintz. I was always sure to find a dish of gossoon pudding, a glass of milk or something of that ilk when I came home evenings. As my room happened

I'M SHAVING MY LOVE FOR YOU!
BLURTED THE SNAKE-CHARMER

The orchestra will now render "The Love Parade," theme song of the motion picture, "The Love Parade," from the play, "The Love Parade," based on the song, "The Love Parade." "What's the charge?" yelped Magistrate Herkimer. "Your Honor, this bloke made a movie showing guys playing marbles for keeps!" Her face was an enigma as she plucked the celery and throatily hummed, "Cooking Gluttons for the One I Love."

THERE'S CROESUS IN MY PANTS, OFFICER! SCREAMED THE TAILOR

And whatever has become of the vaude comic who used to day, "I will now sing you the Soap Song from Lux and after that the Refrain from Smoking"? "Now listen to me, gorilla," thundered the district attorney, "Did you ever keep a saloon?" "Well, not alone," blushed Champagne Charlie, "but I did my bit!" Slip a bromo into my coke, Louie, I gotta pinch a cannon mob in the Ambassador in half an hour.

TAKE OUT THE DUCES AND TRAYS, DANNY, GROWLED THE GAMBLER

Press the buzzard on my desk, Gulliver, and tell Henri to prepare roast vultures with mashed potatoes for ten this evening. "General Gillespie is sick and can't see you today," scowled his orderly. "What made him ill?" squeezed Sergeant Grischball. "Oh, things in general," pulsated the palooka. Don't burn that shoe- maker's Rabelais, Mr. Sumner; the cobbler should stick to his lust.

to be the ice-box, I was not surprised. Often we dined together and ate richly of steamed clamps and humble pie served by Grimes, her obsequious butler. Then we loitered, arm in arm, down Pratt Street past Sprowl, till we reached Undulating Walk. There, 'midst the nostalgic mimosas, the full-lipped aristocrat, her cleft chin a proud banner above her tawny throat, whispered tender pledges into my ears such as cadets have had since the world began. Thus the summer passed away and on its heels—that is, the summer's heels—came autumn and school.

My first four years at Rollins College were uneventful. I was naturally bright and was soon the most popular boy on campus. Rhoda visited me often and made a great hit with the members of my frat.

Then, at the Senior Promenade, I met Edna Fervor. She was a tense little thing, eager, defiant of conventions, sporting a mop of golden hair with which she dusted her dormitory room mornings. Her eyes were twin enigmas as she suavely pledged me in a bumper of mellow hock. I soon learned

CELESTIN VICHY COULD SPIK ENGLISH LAK YOU GURGLED THE GUTTURAL GAUL

The next turn will be an interior decorator on an 18-day diet vo-deo-doing "Am I a Fasting Pansy?" "How do you like your new electric washer, madam?" probed the field agent for Wishy Washers, Inc. "It's poisonous," complained Mrs. Picasso. "Every time I get in, the——paddles bruise my feet!" Maybe I should have sent this one out to the Presbyterian Clinic for a dry clinic·and pressing?

that the was a member of the oldest profession in the world—a linotype operator. Then, like a bolt from the blue, came the fish course and her proposal. Blushing, I promised to become her husband. The stillness of the garden was unbroken, save by the songs of the birds as our lips met. Suddenly I turned to find myself gazing into the flaming eyes of Rhoda Trotwood.

"So this is what I educated you for," she ground bitterly. "Philanderer! Parvenu! Racketeer!" She burst into tears. "To think that I should lose you to this—this——"

"Linotype operator," I stammered weakly.

"Linotype operator?" she shot back icily. "You mean professional bicyclist! Hasn't she told you?" I wheeled aghast on Edna.

"Miss Fervor, is this true?" I demanded wildly. "Are you——?"

"Yes." Her head was bowed. "I was afraid to tell you, Warren; I—I thought you wouldn't understand." I took her in my arms and turned to Rhoda, whose dismay was a mingled picture of rage and mortification.

"I can forgive Edna the past," I told her cuttingly. "But I shall never cease to hate you for attempting to besmirch an innocent girl with your besmircher. Pouf for you!" I snapped my fingers in her crestfallen visage and left her there, suddenly old despite her painted cheeks and false transformation. And so, with Edna's face pressed to mine, I rode out of serfdom. I was a free man again, striking out for a new destiny in fee simple, ready for strong meat and drink and with all the wonder and beauty of Life in my eyes.

I PAINT THE BOATS, BUT BRITANNIA RULES THE WAVES, EXPLAINED REMBRANDT

Kiss me on my tilted coral mouth, Alec, my first hundred thousand before publication has been sold out. "My, what a pretty dimple you have on your chin, darling," bubbled Bashkirtseff. "Aw, that's nothin'," hoarsed little Hatty, aged five, "you should see the one I got on my stomach!" Dussledorf the table, Ludmilla, and put some Berlin water in the tea-caddy; I'm gonna swoon over some fashionable novels this afternoon.

Master Sleuth Unmasked at Last!

All Sherlock Holmes fans sat up in bed with a start last Tuesday and rubbed their eyes in amazement as they scanned the morning papers. After their excitement had abated, they awoke whomever else was in bed and all four promptly telephoned the JUDGE office. From the Battery and the Harlem River Ship Canal, from Follinsbee Road and Pratt Street, from the Boulevard St. Germain, the Friedrichstrasse, and Paddington Heath, haggard-eyed inquiries poured in. Tight-lipped traders on 'Change halted their fevered barter to tensely discuss the astounding revelations. All day long wan operators in the offices of JUDGE heard the same trembling question drift over the wire: "Is Sherlock Holmes really a woman?" The climax of years of research by Pierre de la Matzos had at last borne fruit. The immortal detective stood forth unmasked at last as a member of the perfumed sex (woman).

Meanwhile, in the midst of all this hubbub, Pierre de la Matzos, the French investigator who had raised this tempest in a tea-pot, sat calmly in the Hotel Hubbub in New York. I pushed my way past his horde of secretaries named Beaumont and Fletcherstein and found him quietly reading in his shirt sleeves.

"Ah, Professor Moriarty, I had expected you," he greeted, looking up from reading the gas-meter. "Pray have a chair."

"No, thank you, I already have one," I replied shortly, taking a folding camp-stool from my brief-case and disposing my lanky-knit tweed form upon it. I felt piqued that he had so easily penetrated my disguise of an Indian major retired on half pay.

"I feel piqued that you have so easily penetrated my disguise of an Indian major on half pay," I hinted with just a shadow of pique.

"Elemental, my dear Moriarty, elemental," dismissed de la Matzos, disposing his lanky-knit tweed form on another chair and puffing on his briar. "I knew you were an Indian major directly you refused to have a chair. All Indian majors have chairs. But I say, won't you have a bit of a bloater and a spot of tea?"

"I'd rather have a bit of mackerel, if you have it," I made bold to say.

"Let me see," hesitated de la Matzos, rapidly scanning his fish-tray. "We have pickerel, carperel, percherel, and pikerel, but we're all out of mackerel for the nonce. Maybe if we tried the Board of Education—?"

"But why the Board of Education?" I asked, lighting a nuance.

"For schools of mackerel, you fool," retorted Matzos testily. "Now see here: if you were a mackerel, where would *you* go?"

"Swimming, of course," I replied confusedly.

"But, *mon Dieu*, how can we go swimming?" shrugged he with a typically Gallic gesture. "We have no bathing suits."

"I have—how do you call it?—an undershirt," I suggested hopefully.

"Congratulations," was the acid riposte. "I'll wager you even have a pair of trunks."

"I have, but we keep the hem-stitched towels and the cocktail glasses in them," I admitted ruefully. "Imagine only two closets in a two-room apartment! New York is a great place, but I should certainly hate to live there!"

"But you *do* live in New York, dope," fumed de la Matzos, his eyes twin gimlets above his set mouth. "What's the matter with your memory? You must have lapses."

"No, I'm too fat to have any lapses," I fumbled, slicing the fragrant Cheddar. "But come; I haven't even broached the purpose of my visit."

"Yes, yes," waved Matzos wearily. "You want to know whether it's true that Sherlock Holmes is a woman. Sure he is. His name is really Sheila Holmes, and Dr. Watson used to be governess at Inverness for a mess of a man named Fess. They're all women, every one of them. Why even that Herbert Hoover—did you know he's a graduate of Sweetbriar named Rosa Bonheur and runs a dress shop on the side? They're all women, even me."

"Y-you?" I stammered. "Then—then—will you marry me, Olga?"

"Yes, John," she faltered prettily, blushing like a rose. I took her hands in mine and looked into the mysterious violet pools that were her eyes. Somewhere in the bayou resounded the eerie call of a loon, but we did not pay heed. Gently I and the woman who had once been Olga Nethersole embraced, our

HEY, TAKE THE SHINE OFF MY BLUE SERGE PANTS!" EXPLODED THE INCENSED CUSTOMER

Don't mind that horticulturist yelling, dear; full many a florist is born to bluster unseen. "They tell me the building inspector condemned that mausoleum," remarked the senior member of Sacklow and Asher, Modernistic Morticians. "How come, babe?" grilled Asher. "Aw, there are no fire-escapes on it!" snickered Sacklaw. And if that doesn't develop fifty horsepower, I'll return your Stutz free.

kissers framed in the tangled doorway of the rose-covered cottage. And as the hull of the "Maid of Bombay" disappeared slowly under the horizon, the fierce chant of the Solomon Islands rang out once more over the virgin wilderness. Tonga-Wonga had found her man.

Neo-Einstein Stirs Savants!

"Am I speaking to Professor Motley Throng?"

A tall gentleman with a proud bearing—he explained afterward that his other bearings were at the garage being ground—looked up at my discreet query.

"Why, yes," he smiled infectiously, "I am heel of whom you speak. Come in, if you pleel." I stepped eagerly into the famous inventor's study. One look at Professor Throng confirmed my first impression. He had "class" written all over him; it was scrawled on his nose, his elbow, and even his left leg. I caught my breath between cupped hands and bowed.

"Your servant, Professor Throng," I said smoothly. "I am Conrad Gooly, Photographic Editor of JUDGE. May I have a short statement from you?"

"Certainly," replied the investigator graciously. "How about *'Goldfish are often found surrounded by glass vessels'*?"

"My error, Professor," I apologized. "I should have said I wanted a short statement regarding your new photographic discovery which has set the Thames on fire."

"Oh, you mean my apparatus for developing the film on teeth," replied the Professor, draining his malted milk and giving me a vigorous egg nod. "Well, it all goes back to one night when I was jilted by Irma Voltaire. You knew her, of course?" I mumured assent. Who indeed had not known this regal creature, this woman of the magnificent tawny eyes! Even among mere youths like myself tales were told of this splendid charmer's animal magnetism.

"I had offered her everything I possessed," resumed the Professor. "My shooting preserves in Scotland, my raspberry preserves in Wales, and my candied quinces in Wilkesbarre, Pennsylvania. You knew Pennsylvania, of course?" I murmured assent. Who indeed had not known this splendid state, rich in natural mineral oils and untold lard mines? Even among mere youths like myself tales were told of Pennsylvania, the Mother of Presidents.

"She would have none of me," admitted Professor Throng moodily. "Finally in desperation I offered her two shares in Senator Borah. She blenched; I knew that she was weakening and offered her a course in elementary and advanced Heflin at the State University, with her room rent and tuition free. She was panting. But resolute creature that she was, she would not yield.

"'You cad,' were her only words.

"'You fool,' I threw at her without thinking. I saw her wince. 'Pardon me, your wince is showing,' I added spitefully, my teeth bared in a snarl. She hastily fixed it and turned on me, surveying me intently.

"'Now I can never marry you,' she ground out. 'My wince may show, but who would marry a man with an undeveloped film?'

"That set me thinking, Gooly," went on the Professor without a preamble. "And when—"

"Just a moment, Professor," I interrupted. "Here, have a preamble." The Professor selected one from my pigskin case and lit it thoughtfully, its fragrant clouds filling the room.

"As I say, it set me thinking," he continued. "And when the first faint cracks of dawn came through my window, I just told the dawn to stop its cracks and go home to bed. My problem was solved. I had discovered the Throng Principle of Tooth-Film Photography. In one swell foop—excuse me, in one fell swoop—I had discovered the secret which savants had been questing since the dawn of science."

"Which is?" I gasped, enthralled by the witchery of his word-magic.

"Simply this," boomed the Professor. "That it's all right to get jilted, but you should never get drunk in the process. The process is no place to get

HOW WOULD YOU LIKE A KREES IN YOUR PANTS, BABY?
MOUTHED THE MALICIOUS MALAY

Care to buy a nice Swiss watch, mister? Me and my pal here had to knife a guy to get it. "Hey, don't shoot, your gun ain't loaded!" bawled a Nimrod to his excited friend in the duck-bout. "Can't help that, the bird won't wait!" gibbered the yap. Just for that, Benny, you go home and write a dirty word on your Pappy's bald head five hundred times.

drunk. Somebody else may want to get in there while you stay locked in, selfishly keeping everybody on tenterhooks outside. Stay out of the process and the pennies will take care of themselves. And now, young man, I will ask you to leave, first having returned to me that fly-paper you've been sitting on since you came in here.''

Which is the true and unvarnished reason why I happened to be walking down Evans Street without any pants on last Monday afternoon.

Flat-Footers Frisk Fiddler's Flat!

Hearts beat faster the world over last night when Ernest Heminway, president of the Ernest Heminway Wrecking Company, which is tearing down the Fritz Chrysler, announced to reporters that he had discovered the "Barcarole" from the "Tales of Hoffman" lodged near the 56th floor. From Tia Juana to Tomsk, from Brest-Litovsk to Bounty Bay, from Lithuania to the Leeward Islands, wherever tattooed hands grasp glasses of grog, King Bewilderment reigned supreme. In low boozing-kens in Limehouse Reach and evil notch-joints in Port Said, the riff-raff of the Seven Seas stared at each other in stupefaction. Swarthy Lascars and sneering Eurasians in the crooked purlieus of the Forbidden City blenched at the news and barricaded themselves in their hovels, hastily flinging pocket moats about them for protection. In the snowy summits of monasteried Tibet slant-eyed priests spun prayer-wheels with palsied hands and burned special joss-sticks labeled "Crowell Publishing Company" before their idols. Even in Virginia among the stately mansions, the courtly fops, the gracious belles, and the tasty food served amid homelike surroundings at reasonable prices, terror and astoundment fought with each other.

"Gad, sir!" puffed one elderly red-faced colonel on the levee at Natchez, tugging at his white imperial, "Ah kain't remember anything like this since fearless Beauregard leaped with his guerrillas into the breach at Shiloh! What next?"

"Just this, Colonel Yancy," retorted Cameo Kirby, a gentleman gambler who had been fingering the delicate silk ruffles at his wrists, "I'll wager you five thousand they'll find 'Anitra's Dance' from the Peer Gynt Suite before morning!"

"Done, suh!" cried Yancy, giving the gambler his hand. A moment later a picturesque blackamoor who had been asleep on a bale of cotton raced toward them with a telegram. Yancy tore it open impatiently. It was from the Ernest Heminway Wrecking Company.

"Discovered 'Anitra's Dance' from Peer Gynt Suite in the Chrysler appendix," read the gambler. "Have just uncovered 'Fifth Hungarian Rhapsody' of Brahms arranged for the clavichord in the clavicle."

Meanwhile, in New York, a raiding party of police broke into Fritz Chrysler's apartment and discovered the bones of a baton and a half-eaten spinet. The remains were shown to the spinet's mother, who identified them as Franz Liszt. At this moment, however, Franz Liszt entered arm-in-arm with Rudy Beethoven.

"What's all this?" he demanded indignantly. "How dare you upset Chrysler's apartment? Have you got a license?" The police captain showed him a document marked "License to Upset Chrysler's Apartment" and explained the situation.

"Rubbish!" exploded Beethoven. "Why, this is Liszt right here! We've just come from eating Fritz himself!"

"I'll tell the world," added Liszt. "He was delicious! And the chestnut dressing—yum yum!"

"But listen, men," expostulated the police captain. "Are you sure it was Chrysler? I saw him myself being torn down this morning over at the Ernest Heminway Wrecking plant." The two composers went white.

"Quick, Franz, there's not a moment to be lost!" shouted Beethoven, dropping his pen on his unfinished symphony. "Pray God we're in time to save him from those hell-cats!" In a moment they were in a fiacre speeding toward the Heminway plant. Their carriage had hardly drawn to the steps when a horrified employee clutched at their coat-tails.

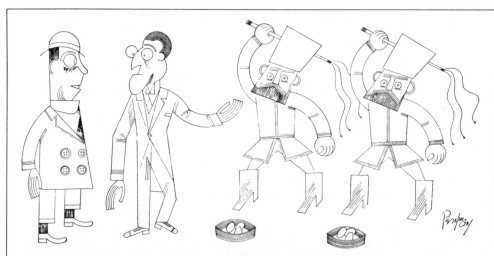

HERE'S SOMETHING CUTE IN EGG-BEATERS! FLOURISHED THE FLOOR-WALKER

Will one of you little momzers ask Lord Shrubley to wipe the pathos from his face before going into the bathos? "You're a locksmith, are you?" scathed the sergeant. "What were you doing in that gambling joint we just pulled?" "I was making a bolt for the door," trembled the trash. Since Lord and Taylor told the gals it's smart to be shifty, none of 'em will even look you in the eye.

YOU CAN LEAD A HORSE TO VASSAR BUT YOU CAN'T MAKE HER THINK!! STORMED THE DEAN

The Four Revelling Paper-Hangers in their stirring song mask, "Oh, How I'd Love to See That Old Kalsomine." "Who's that fat cove you just spoke to?" snapped the senior member of Bolabosta and Balbatooney, Boiled Birds' Bones by the Box or Bushel. "I dunno, I didn't get near enough to him to catch his name!" jittered the cluck. And then, of course, there were the days when you wore "I'm the Guy" buttons and thought "Let's not and say we did!" was wit.

I'M UP A GREEK WITHOUT A PADDLE
FLUTTERED THE PHONEY BOLONEY

Meet our two best basketball players, girls, Red House and Swollen Glantz, a couple of hard centers from Maillard Prep. "Who are you, mugg?" pouted the prom trotter. "I'm a Rutgers man, lady," mumbled the pig's trotter. "Well, go upstairs and sleep it off," buzzed Thirty-Per-Cent-Off-for-Pash. Hang up your clothes in the stevedore, gob; you're in the navvy now.

"Mr. Beethoven, Mr. Liszt!" he stammered, "Scribner's Sons have just eaten Mr. Heminway!" He pointed toward the roof where Scribner's sons were leering at them. In a flash Liszt had drawn his derringer and fired from the hip. The taut bystanders saw Scribner's Sons waver, clutch the parapet, and slide down the steep incline, just as Edna Ferber and Mary Roberts Rinehart drove up in another fiacre.

"Thank Heaven you arrived in time, boys," gasped Miss Ferber. "Those beasts have just stolen Thornton Wilder and Fannie Hurst!"

"It was only a prank," snuffled Scribner's Sons at their feet. "We won't do it again, honest!" They were let off with a severe reprimand and were turned over to Horace Liveright to be flogged. Then, with many a hearty oath and foul innuendo, the party piled into the New York Times Book Review and were driven off the end of a wharf. Spring had come to Tin Pan Alley.

Commencement Exercises

Members of the Graduating Class of The College of Tree Surgery:

When Professor Cockroft of the Trunk and Roots Department approached me to award the diplomas at your commencement exercises, I felt somewhat embarrassed, principally because I had left the bathroom door open and the steam was so thick I couldn't see who it was. To make matters worse, the soap slipped out of reach, and when I made a pass for it, I got hold of Professor Cockroft's ankle, which is no bargain—ha, ha, ha.

Four years of your carefree student life have been passed and you stand today on the threshold of the sea of Life, ready to chart unknown dangers and mount the ladder of Success. To you, young men, I would say: Do not waver under the buffets of Disappointment, but let Experience take you by the hand, and turn your back on Lust and Evil Companions. I often think of Life as a stage on which we are only players; to each one is it given to speak his small piece and then vanish from the scene. As you make your way through the forest of Knowledge, arm yourself with the tweezers of Courage and the saw of Determination and leap lightly over the hurdles of Disillusionment, watching carefully lest your untrained feet become snared by those lurking roots of Defeat, Smoking and Loose Women. When your head is bowed by the weight of cares, let a smile be your umbrella, 'neath Fate's tempest.

If my son came to me and said, "Father, what profession would you advise me to take up? I am thinking of becoming a hop-head," I would take his head in my hands, and say, "Son (or daughter, as the case may be), have you thought about tree surgery? Let me tell you a story. One day, when I was one-

and-twenty, I was walking in the woods. Suddenly I heard a little stifled moan coming from a furze-bush. There in the gloaming, boykins, was a poplar sapling with a thorn in its foot, gazing dumbly at me and making appealing little forest noises. In a trice I whipped out my kit and extracted the thorn. Then I went my way, boy o' mine, and forgot the incident. Several hours later I was startled by a fierce growl in a thicket. A huge, shaggy water-buffalo, its fangs bared, was preparing to leap on me. I cowered back in alarm; the beast jumped and I thought my days were numbered. But it was not to be. To my surprise, the grateful poplar sapling threw itself between us and crushed the puffalo to a bulp—the buppalo to a fulf—the fuppalo to a bulf—well, he just

HUSH MONEY PAPA'S BRIBING THE BULLS QUICKLY QUIETED MRS. QUILT

It may not be easel, but I'll fixatif you ink it's the best way out. "Charming place this," barked Mellish to Hellish as they strolled through the rooms of Monticello. "See the old wing?" "Yeh, had it for lunch yesterday," maundered the momzer.

smashed that old water-buffalo, let me tell you. I took the sapling home with me, and in time our friendship ripened into love. That little sapling, laddies, was—your mother.''

Tonight, at your class supper, you will join arms for the last time to sing your Alma Mater's stirring old marching song, ''Teak for Two.'' Then your paths will separate; some of you will become juniper men, others will specialize on beeches and larches. But at heart you will all be sons of the old school, ready to saw a limb off each other as you would off a patient. You may not all of you have been brilliant in twigonometry, but you can all climb like monkeys and are practially indistinguishable from them in a dim light. March on with good fellowship in your hearts, men, and make that reunion five years hence something to be remembered as you return covered with chestnut blight, both legs gone, and a hole in your head as large as a soup tureen. And if you don't come back at all, the rest of us will have an even better time. Nuts to you, my fine fellows.

Oh, That Dirty Photograph Business!

This morning, whilst teasing my beard in the Rose Room of Monticello, my summer home, with Baffles, my man, at every beck and turn—excellent fellow, Baffles, none better at taking care of my becks and turns, though he does steal my thunder now and then, I'm sure I caught him wiping his lips when I came in from hounds the other afternoon—perhaps I'd better begin this sentence over again. As I say, this morning whilst meditating in the Blue-Jay Room of my shooting box in Scotland, I happened to shake my head and a small object fell out of my beard. On closer examination it turned out to be one of those fake photographs named ''*S.S. Leviathan*, showing Comparative Relation of This Floating Palace to the Woolworth Building.'' You probably have one of the damn things in your trunk right now while you're reading this—no, you probably haven't got a trunk, or you wouldn't be sitting in a barber-shop over this journal; you'd be at home shaving yourself. Well, anyway, I fell to musing over this quaint old picture, sipping my glass of port and adjusting my tippet, and my reverie carried me back to old days in the A.E.F. when I was stationed at Gateau-sur-Marne—we were getting out a paper called *The Stars and Stripes* then—and first thing I knew I woke up and looked in the *Mirror*, and who do you suppose I had turned into? Alexander Woollcott! Mercy me, here we are at the end of the first paragraph and we haven't even gotten down to biz. Tut, tut and Mr. Tutt, I think I can hear that arthur train whistling at the crossing already.

Talk about street-grooms going out of business since horseless carriages came in and corset-makers starving since corsets went out—they're nothing. The men who paste together those scale pictures of steamers and skyscrapers haven't eaten a square meal since 1913. In case you're thinking of putting up a tablet to these unsung heroes, the date is September 12th, 1913. On that day Harvey Gaffney, of the firm of Young, Stripling & Co., Scale Photographers, was called into Mr. Stripling's private office.

"Take off your hat. Do you think you're in a saloon?" greeted Mr. Stripling. Gaffney reached into Mr. Stripling's vest pocket, selected a Havana and bit one end off.

"You shouldn't talk to me that way," he said mildly. "If I wanted to tell your wife how you and Miss Wetzel in the outer office—"

"Now, Harvey, please," began Mr. Stripling in a choking voice, "I only thought maybe—"

"Never mind what you *thought*!" shouted Gaffney suddenly. "What do you want? What's the idea of breaking into my afternoon nap with your stories?"

"I—I just got a phone call from downtown." stammered Mr. Stripling. "They got a new building down there, Harvey—it's called the Woolworth Building. I—I thought maybe you'd like to go down there and compare it with the *Leviathan*."

"Why don't you send down one of your cheap twenty-dollar-a-week slobs?" bawled Gaffney. "*I* should drag myself down there—"

"Harvey," said Mr. Stripling in a low, tempting voice, producing a Northern Spy apple from his desk, "Oh, Harvey! Look what I got, harvey, I got one for you too, Harvey, if you go down and see that building. Hey, Harvey?"

"What kind of apple will mine be?" demanded Harvey suspiciously.

"It's a Ridgefield Pippin, Harvey," wheedled Mr. Stripling. "Look, all for you, Harvey." Harvey's eyes lit up and he gave way. Harvey was a sucker for Ridgefield Pippins, all right, all right.

Well, Harvey had just come out of the subway in front of the Woolworth Buil-

I'M JUST A SLAV TO MY PASSIONS, LADY, PROTESTED THE MUSCOVITE
I wonder whether that jar of hard candies I just ate could have been bath salts? Whoops, that reminds me. "Young man, young man!" called impatient old Mrs. Hosmer to the clerk of the confectionery store. "What is it, ma'am?" queried Oiving politely. "Who waits on the nuts here?" demanded La Hosmer, stamping her foot. If the snow is afraid of the sunshine, what would the atmos-phere?—ha ha!

ding when he saw a pert miss ahead of him. She had the most beautiful eyes Harvey had ever seen, and straightaway Harvey fell head over heels in love. In ten days they were engaged to be married. The day of the wedding she came to him with swollen eyes.

"Why, what is the matter, Ingeborg?" demanded her swain.

"I must tell you everything!" she sobbed. "I am not what you think me. My father is—'Get-Rich-Quick-Wallingford!'"

"Then you are—" he blanched.

"Blackie Daw," she said brokenly. "I play a sax when I am alone."

With a hoarse cry Harvey ran into the night. There was no way out. He hastened to Mrs. Stripling and told her of her husband's intrigue with Miss Wetzel in the outer office. Mrs. Stripling was so wroth she made Stripling give up his share in the scale photograph business and become a switch-master of a Lionel electric train. And since this happened to be the only firm in the world dealing in scale photographs, you can imagine what the life of a scale photographer had been since then. So I say to you, young men of the North Braintree School of Business Administration: live loosely but not well, take care of your pennies and the dog pound will take care of you, and look forward to the time when I'm walking and you're riding in a limousine. And I hope it's an ambulance.

NOW LET'S TAKE IT ON THE LAMB QUICK! SAID THE PHOTOGRAPHER

Here's the one we mopped with in the deuce spot at the Elite in Scoharie last fall. "Why didn't he rent you his apartment, Jake?" asked Jake. "He said I was so bow-legged that I'd always be rubbing the paper off the walls, Jake!" responded Jake. Oh, Mr. Shubert, you're not going to send me on the road?

The Wolf in the Servidor

There has been such an avalon of letters the past two days whining for me to break silence on the Bamberger-Watkins wolf case that I would be a heel indeed to keep my lips sealed. Only this morning a round robin flew in the window, signed by the Chubby Bus-Boys' Union, Local 119, of Batavia, Ill., demanding "Are you seal enough to keep your lips heeled on this burning question, viz., the Bamberger-Watkins wolf case?" Who so flinty as to turn a deaf ear to a chubby bus-boy? What churlish deaf-ear turner so callous that he could remain stony before this winsome appeal?

It all started Tuesday in the office of King James Versian, general manager of the Hotel Pennsylvania. Mr. Versian's office, richly simple in tone, was luxurial in the extreme; daft Seminoles flitted about noiselessly waiting on our whim whilst we dawdled over our root beers discussing the new tariff arriving next Sunday to take charge of the synagogue. It was a scene of indescribable splendoom. Suddenly Ridgely Simple, one of the assistant managers, appeared at Mr. Versian's elbow and whispered something into it.

Only 1,964 baths?" roared Versian. "What's become of the other 236? Are you trying to play hub with our motto, '2,200 rooms, 2,200 baths'?"

"L-lots of the guests swipe souvenirs," stammered Simple. "Maybe one of the bell-hops stole—"

"Come, come, Semple," snarled Versian.

"Simple, sir," corrected the young man with quiet dignity.

"Oh, verts," sputtered Versian. "Between you and me, wasn't it Julius Galitzianer before you shortened it? Why not call a spade a spade?"

"What spade, sir?" asked Simple stupidly. Before Versian could reply, "Carrots," the red-headed irrepressible

DOES OO LOVE LI'L HENRYKINS? INQUIRED THE FRESH THING.

Hello, little radio fans, this is Uncle Frankie, about to bend your ear again with his kilocycles. A little ape accosted his granpa once and said, "Hey, fish-face, make a noise like a frog, will you?" "Why, Eglantine?" inquired the bewildered oldster. "Because the pater says that when you croak we'll get five thousand smackers!" was the astounding answer. Mush on, malamutes, we've to get that diphtheria serum to Nome tonight.

office-boy, put his head in.

"Hully gee, boss," he said, "dey's a felly outside wid a message fer yez. Shall I show de bloke in?"

"Show him in, 'Carrots,'" ordered Mr. Versian instantly. "And I'll show him up." We had scarcely finished laughing at this shaft when a scarlet-faced gentleman swept in.

"I'm Bamberger," he began. "When am I going to get my wolf back?"

"Your wolf?" demanded Versian helplessly.

"You heard me, my wolf!" bawled Bamberger. "I put him in the servidor this morning to be dry-cleaned, and now they won't give him back before tomorrow night. I got to open with him in Wilmington tomorrow night or I lose seventeen thousand smackers!"

"Open?" queried Versian slowly. "Open what?"

"The safe in the Delaware Oyster Company," explained Bamberger. "He helps me carry my tools."

"Tell me," interrupted Versian, "did you put your wolf in a bag when you placed him in the servidor?"

"Sure I did," admitted Bamberger.

"Well, he's 'in the bag,'" all right, all right." laughed Versian. "He probably got sent to the laundry by mistake!"

"But he isn't washable!" screamed Bamberger. "He'll shrink! I'll sue—"

"No, you won't," cut in Versian. "There's a sign on your dresser whiuch says clearly, 'All shrinkable wolves laundered at owner's risk.' Well, 'Carrots,'" what is it now?"

"Faix, boss," simmered "Carrots" excitedly, "dey's anudder shpalpeen out here by de name ob Watkins wants ter see yez." He was brushed aside by an indignant tight-lipped gentleman with dark glasses.

"They gave me the wrong wolf!" he bellowed. "I give a wolf to the valet to be sponged and pressed and now they want to ring in some motheaten hyena on me!"

"Listen, mugg, you'll eat those words!" barked Bamberger menacingly.

"Oh, you're the clown that owns that mangy old lap-robe, hey?" sneered Watkins derisively, advancing on Bamberger. We rushed at them to tear them apart when Versian put his finger up to

EVERY LITTLE NOOK IN GRANNY HAS A MEANING ALL ITS OWN SAID FRITZ

Needles to say, it is easier to thread a camel than to put the cart before the horse. "Yes, ma'am, this is the composing-room," indicated Ichabod, Prince of Printers and jolly good fellow withal. "Isn't that thrilling!" fluttered Freda, "Won't you sing something you've composed recently, Mr. Valspar?"

his lips.

"Hush, men," he said softly, "They're dancing." We recoiled, chop-fallen. It was true; their feet were moving nimbly through the smooth, dreamy intricacies of the waltz issuing from the sobbing violins in the Lefkowitz Lounge. What fools we had been not to realize that Watkins was really a girl dressed in boy's clothes! One by one we tiptoed cautiously from the room, leaving Ives Bamberger alone to plight his throat with Velma Watkins. Somewhere in the glen the poignant sweetness of an avocado sounded high above the noise of the grackles. The skirling of the war-pipes was hushed; the spears of the Bamberger and Watkins clans had fallen before the bow of Cupid, the roguish God of Love.

Do You Stuff Turkeys, Mister?

About October 15th the moon will be in Virgo, Uranus will be in the ascendant, Sagittarius will be well on the wane from looking thru too many keyholes, and Mrs. Feinberg, in the apartment below, will have finished hammering in nails with her husband's best military hair-brushes. Between then and January 1st (when Mrs. Feinberg will open the winter season by hammering nails in her husband) all you little leeches will be very, very busy indeed getting ready for Thanksgiving. I have been running around, like a head with its chicken cut off, making lists of things you'll need for Thanksgiving dinner. Well, sir, it's finally finished and drawn up by Fitz and Stotz, my attorneys, in collaboration with Mr. Ford Madox Hoofer, the English tap-dancer, and here it is. Sorry you had to wait so long for it.

First, of course, comes the quetion of wiring the turkey. No, no, not wiring the turkey to come to the dinner; plenty of turkeys will come without being wired. I mean fixing the time bomb inside him, so that when you throw the switch under the table he can explode right in your Uncle Prouty's face. This is something of an art. Take last year's dinner, for instance; the damn thing exploded without even singeing Uncle Prouty's beard. All you did was throw a horrible fright into the poor fowl and a gravy-spoon into Aunt Sigrid's decolletage. A handful of ground glass in the sage dressing, plenty of nitroglycerine around the roast potatoes, and leave the rest to Edison. When you see those internes giggling as they brush Uncle's chestnut-covered parts into a galvanized pail, you'll feel glad you took all that trouble. Not to mention Saint Peter's chuckles when he enters "Thursday—one mealy gent named Prouty with cranberry sauce" in his ledger. Come clean, now; how many times has Mamma asked you to be nice to Uncle Prouty? Be nice to him? Why, you'll send him home in stitches!

WELL, HERE'S A PRETTY KETTLE OF FITCH INDEED! SNARLED MRS. FITCH

December thirteenth and still the only mugg in the biz who hasn't popped a miniature golf or baby Austin jape. "They tell me you're quite a nautical man, Captain Creplach," simpered Miss Simpson. "Yes," drawled the old chozzer with a twinkle, "I know every schooner around San-Francisco!" I bet the kind of a "schooner" he meant had plenty of foam around it, har, har, har.

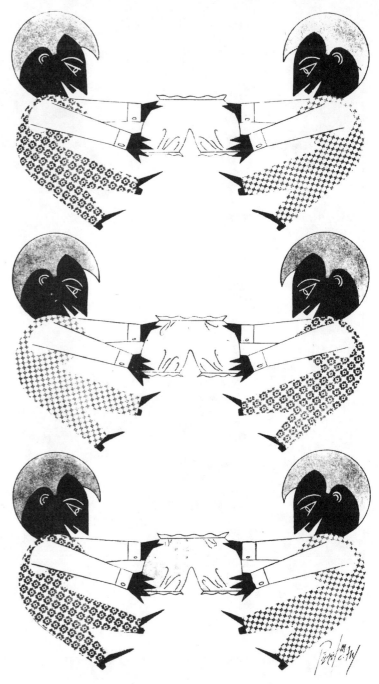

**WE'RE PULLING SOME AWFUL BLOOMERS!
STUTTERED THE SABLE SEXTET**

Foreign sahib like to see peep-show like U.S.A., only real hotstuff? This way, plizz. "Now, what insect lives on the least food?" demanded the chief bug-crafter of the Kibitzer Patrol. "The moth, it eats holes!" attested Tenderfoot Nussbaum, twisting a tourniquet. Mortar, stop pestling your Papa or I'll give you with the belt in the boom-boom!

What are you mumbling there in the corner? Oh, so that's it, hey? You haven't an Uncle Prouty! Well, what have you done with him? Speak up! Got mislaid, did he?... Well, all right, I'll let you go this time, but I ought to search you just the same. That's what comes of letting boys wear a bib and play with teddy-bears. Never saw any of MY young 'uns turn into mealy-mouthed cheats, I wager! No, suh, I send 'em off to Peddie when they're eleven, suh; teach 'em bracing manly games! Make 'em sturdy little beggars, suh, that's the old Army rule, let 'em ride without blanket and surcingle, without even a horse! Two sons in the Coast Artillery, suh, and one at old Fort Jonathan Wayde, guarding their Flag. And when that blood-red sun sinks over the ramparts, suh, with the bugle playing Reveille and the wind soughing in the pines, suh, and the regimental band playing "*I Scream—You Scream—We All Scream for Ice Cream*," well, suh, I just want to say you can have all your French sauces and your peppery curries, but just give me a dish of good old marinierte herring with cold boiled potato wrapped up in the Flag, and if those dirty Bolsheviks want to tear down our institutions and ideals they can go right back where they came from. Yes, siree, they can take it right from their old tobacco-chawin', whittlin', no-account Uncle Jonathan, by gum! Because when a Cape Codder's said his say, neighbor, it's *said*. We gave boneless codfish cakes and Coolidge to the nation, mister, and they can't laugh that off, I reckon. We may look hard as flint on the surface, Mister New York City Slicker, but daown deep we's jest chillun; jest as tender as a blacksnake whip. Only not so beautiful.

Phrenology—Yes or No?

Some years ago, whilst I was travelling in the southern part of the United States and lecturing on phrenology, I was overtaken by a severe thunderstorm and compelled to seek refuge from the elements—fire, earth, water, hydrogen, idoform, and cuneiform—in a lovely farmhouse. Mine host, bluff Squire Turgeniev, had two beautiful daughters named Grace, shapely young blondes of about nineteen years old apiece, with dazzling blue eyes and even teeth. We spent the evening talking about phrenology, and all through the conversation I could feel the burning eyes of the girls upon me. When the time came to retire, I discovered much to my dismay that there were only twelve beds available, as a platoon of Union soldiers was quartered in the buttery under Major Yancy and there was a band of lawless gorillas bivouacking in the scullery. This meant that I would have to put up in the constabulary among the horses. I withdrew there with good grace and wrapped myself in my tartan. In a few moments I was in the arms of Morpheus, so to speak. I must have slept an hour or so when a timid knock on the door aroused me. Buckling on my buckler, I answered the door cautiously, thinking that it was one of

Yancy's troops. To my amazement, it turned out to be the eldest of Squire Turgeniev's daughters, a comely brunette scarcely turned twenty, in whose imperious eyes I beheld the untamed spirit of Viking ancestors and sea-rovers.

"I—I have mislaid my harp," she stammered prettily beneath downcast cheeks. "Can you help me?" Ever a ladies' man, this bewitching appeal could not fail to move me. I looked about, but with the exception of a harp named Shamus O'Donnell, asleep in the straw, I could see nothing which answered her description.

"Oh, don't bother, sir," she interrupted nervously. "I really came here to ask you something. I have been a lover of good horse-flesh since infancy, but every time I go near a horse it kicks. Would you examine my skull and see whether phrenology can find the answer?"

I immediately put on my shoes and subjected the crown of her head to a close examination. There lay the answer indeed. The small bump, "Capable of Subduing High-Spirited Colts," was missing. She blenched when I told her, and great tears gathered in her magnificent orbs. I advised her to seek out some other profession, preferably in some city where there was a paucity of horses. A hasty consultation of MacGregor's Horse Index revealed that Mound City, Missouri, possessed only three horses, two of whom had mulish tempers. Wrapping my tartan about both of us, we quickly drove off in her father's racing gig. Today the young lady is happily married to a pastry cook named Furniss and she tends the Furniss with her own loving hands. Peace to her ashes.

I have told this short and stuffy story to make clear just what help phrenology can be. In this connection I recall an anecdote illustrating a more poignant side of the science. Several years ago I was overtaken by a violent drought whilst on my way to Tombstone, Arizona, to give myself up. I was forced to take shelter for the night in the home of bluff Squire Furniss. After a hearty supper, the

HEY MIND YOUR OWN DARN BISMUTH RETORTED THE BIG-TIME RETORTER

You should have seen the brace of grice—the brice of grouse—oh, what a bunch of turkeys I shot yesterday! Here's one: "Gimme change for a dime, please," mumbled Mr. Meecham. "Here y'are," droned the druggist, "and I hope you enjoy the sermon!" The Kangaroo's waistline will fit smugly above the hips this fall, with the usual patch pockets featured.

bluff squire and his charming young wife, a ravishing brunette with enticing curves and melting eyes, besieged me with questions about phrenology. All evening I felt the squire's burning eyes fixed upon me. Came bedtime and I found to my consternation that the barn had burned down and I would have to sleep in the house. Wrapping myself in a plain wrapper, I lay down under my bed and prepared to woo Dame Slumber. A moment later a soft knock aroused me. There in the doorway stood the squire, smiling mysteriously, his hands holding something I could not see.

"Why, what have you there?" I asked, bewildered.

"It's a box for you, honey," he replied.

"A box? What kind of box?" I stuttered.

"A box on the nose, you —— you!" shouted the squire, and he hit me with some sort of blunt instrument like a telegraph pole. I had just enough time to dodge out by the side door and help his wife into the waiting buckboard. In a few moments we had oustripped the squire. We were married in the next town by a sleepy minister. The squire's rage soon abated and he begged us to come home for his forgiveness.

Today the three of us live happily in the old house beneath the immemorial elms. As I sit here, nodding over my embroidery in the hot sunshine, I hear Jared's footsteps behind me. Still erect and soldierly, despite the ravages of sixty summers, he strokes my graying hair with his firm brown hand. And as we stand together by the honeysuckles, listening to the merry cries of the milkmaids rolling in the gloaming, we both think back down Memory Lane to the brave, bright days of '61 when youth's heart beat high and a little Southern belle's lips pledged her love to dashing Jared Paderewski of the Massachusetts Volunteers.

The Grit of the Peagraves

"But, Bertha, why shouldn't you marry Wayne Peagrave?" Professor Leopold Bloom patted his daughter's fine-spun hair affectionately. "I'm sure he's a very good student; in fact, he's the best man in my class!"

"Oh, Dad!" Bertha Bloom's voice was impatient and there was a flash of rebellion in those clear topaz eyes, inherited from centuries of Jewish warrior ancestors who had fallen in the Crusades into easy jobs. "Can't you understand? How can I marry a man who's yellow?"

"Listen, baby, *you* should talk about skin pigments?" demanded her father severely. "You're only a jump from the Arabs yourself. And the Arabs and the Chinks all come from the same basket."

"Oh, Dad, you *are* a bookworm!" scoffed Bertha in mock despair. "What I mean is, Wayne's a quitter! He promised me he'd make his hockey letter or die in the attempt. And you know I'd never marry a man who's done nothing for old Chiropractic Tech," she finished firmly.

"Come, come," soothed Professor Bloom. "There speaks your grandfather. Gad, what a man! You know, on his mother's side he was a Rothschild, with his mouth closed," he added proudly.

"What was he with it open?" asked Bertha sullenly.

"A gorilla," admitted the Professor sadly. "A plain, ordinary gorilla, just like you. But here it is ten o'clock and your mother told me she wanted to have a talk with you this evening."

"Say, have I got to listen to another one of those so-the-little-bee-carries-the-pollen-from-one-flower-to-another spiels?"groaned Bertha."Why doesn't that dame catch wise to herself? Listen, I could show her a book—"

"Never mind, Bertha, now," interrupted her father. "Run along." And he returned his absorbed glance to the Decameron, the great scientific work to which he was dedicating his life.

Meanwhile, Wayne Peagrave, the subject of all this disclosure, moodily hunched his shoulders deep into his collegiate topcoat and faced the biting wind which swept down Pratt Street. Rain flicked its lash across his finely chiseled features as he recalled what she had said when he had asked her to be Bertha Peagrave. Could a fellow help it if his ankles buckled every time he stood up on a pair of skates? Hadn't he tried, hadn't he gritted his teeth, remembering his ancestors who had rushed into the enemy's guns at Jutland, Schastopol, Chicamunga, Austerlitz, Ticonderoga, the Battle of the Boyne, Hastings, Salamis, and Thermopylae? As he neared the dormitory of Mordaunt Hall he thrust his jaw pugnaciously forward. He'd show her! Nobody'll call a Peagrave a quitter! His "roomie," Erskine Burbage, who was out on a date, looked up in surprise as he entered and threw himself, brooding heavily, upon the bed. One by one the lights of Mordaunt Hall disappeared, but still Wayne Peagrave stared with furrowed

WE'LL HAVE A NICE ROAST TURNKEY FOR DINNER, BOYS
CLOWNED EAST NEW YORK LOUIE

Wanted—A bloke with a steady hand to stencil new fall model eyebrows on Greta Garbo. "Hey, I want the life of Caesar!" fumed a freshman, tapping on the librarian's desk. "Sorry, babe," jibed the junior, "Brutus beat you to it!" Or, as the Pekinese said to his girl friend, "I may be Wong, but I think you're wonderful!"

brows at Bertha's picture.

The temporary bleachers which had been erected around Ezra Pond for the annual hockey contest with Dismukes University were filled with impatient rooters of both factions eagerly awaiting the fray. Gaily attired co-eds with sparkling cheeks and red eyes waved pennants and shouted lusty accompaniment to the cheerleader's hoarse requests for a long C-h-i-r-o-p-r-a-c-t-i-c for the team. In reply the Dismukes cohorts took up the chorus:

"Dismukes, Dismukes, Mother o' Men,
'Neath thy elms time immemorial
Recalls us to thy banner armorial,
So it's fight, fellows, and put up your dukes
For one-two-three-four-five and old Dismukes!"

In the Dismukes' locker-room the coach was facing his tense charges with stern mien, giving them their final instructions. They were so intent upon his words that none of them heard a light footfall in an adjoining room where the skates were stored. Wayne Peagrave, masked and closely drawing a black cloak around his figure, had entered cautiously. He had timed it perfectly. It was but the work of a moment to draw the oxyacetylene torch from its folds. One by one he held the skates of the opposing team in the intense flame till they were at white heat. Then, as quickly as he had come, he slipped through the window.

The referee's whistle was poised; the request of the Dismukes team that the wool be drawn over their ice to clean it had been complied with; and now the puck was flung from President Imbrie's hand and was skimming over the ice. Away went both teams, their skates clicking shrilly. But, alas, for Chiropractic's hopes—their team was outnumbered ten to one. Black despair settled over their supporters as they saw victory going to the invading Dismukians. But what was this? Something was happening to the ice beneath the conquerors' feet! One after the other felt the ice melting as he tried to grip the surface with his white-hot skates. Slowly the whole team was hopelessly bogged, attempting vainly to extricate itself! A new figure darted out in the mauve-and-cobalt uniform of Chiropractic. Why, it was Wayne Peagrave, substituting for Grosgrain Katz, Chiro's injured forward! The Tech stands were on their feet, mad with joy. Sure-footed, he swiftly led the exultant players into the ranks of Dismukes and wreaked havoc with his devastating shinny-stick. Then, leaving the unconscious and crestfallen invaders prone on the ice, he planted his flag in the very heart of Dismuke's territory as the final whistle blew. Chiropractic had won, seven to four!

It was a proud and moist-eyed Bertha who snuggled against the gray-and-saffron "C" of Wayne's sweater and promised to change her name to Peagrave for better or for worse as they were borne from Ezra Pond by their jubilant classmates.

"Oh, Wayne, darling, I knew you could do it!" she breathed happily. Her lover, busily signing vaudeville, movietone, and book contracts, sighed contentedly.

"All I want is you, honey," he said tenderly. "You beside me in front of the fire reading extracts from that book your father is writing, and let the rest of the world peddle its papers!'" And as the triumphal bonfires of Old Chiro burned low, Wayne Peagrave and his betrothed looked deep into each other's eyes and found there that secret which only Youth, in the fragrance-laden sweetness of the lilacs, can know.

Special Dispatch from the Moroccan Front

Sidi-Bel-Abbes, Morocco, Dec. 10.—Not since Caesar's Garlic Legions left Cisalpine Gaul (Book IV, Page 79) has there been anything like this war with the Riffs. First I should like my good friends in Lithuania, who are all grouped around the stove in Uncle Vaslavya's store, to know that I arrived safely here in America last Tuesday according to the Julian Calendar who meet me at the boat and pin a green ticket on my reefer. Well, I already got good job driving truck, the people puts things they don't need any more on the sidewalk and we lift those articles on truck one, two, three. Then we pile everything on scow and she steam out to twelve-mile limit, where motorboats bring them in again and sells them to the people at good prices. It is called "Prohibition." I bet Anastasia Vitebsk will get passionate over my picture I send next month of me in white uniform with badge and brush. New York is fine place, they use gold in the teeth here instead of wood pegs like in Lithuania and everybody selling good juicy eating apples for five cents on the corner. It is called "Prosperity." Everything has a name here.

So here we are in Morocco trying to get started on this war, only between the movie cameras and the sound technicians no enemy has showed up. Worse than that, nobody seems to know who owns the Foreign Legion; a Metro-Goldwyn-Mayer director had a fist-fight with a Paramount electrician who claimed his company had bought it for 200 bolivars Brazilian money in 1924. The M-G-M man got in a good bust on the other's nose and everything was going fine until somebody discovered the sound machine wasn't working. So they had to do three retakes and you should have seen that electrician's hook.

Friday night some of the Legionnaires were yawning in the bunkhouse waiting for Captain Pettibone to bring them their hot milk and knishes when one of the regimental musicians heard a scraping noise in his zither. An investigation proved that there was a Riff in his lute. There was some question about how he was going to be tied when captured; Universal Pictures suggested he sign one of their contracts, but the prisoner put up a fearful battle. At length, however, he signed, and bound hand and foot, he was hauled before the drumhead court-martial. At first the Riff confessed he was a powder-monkey named Jim Hawkins, claimed he had secreted himself in the apple-barrel to overhear the mutineers' plans. When cross-hatched by the opposing attorney, Hawkins wavered.

"How do you account for there being no apples in the barrel when we found you?" scowled Law-Tycoon Trelawney.

"I ate them," stammered Hawkins, adding bitterly, "I wish I had eaten the barrel."

"But it wasn't a barrel, it was a lute," pursued the lawyer.

"What do you mean a lute, who ever heard of apples in a lute?" sneered Hawkin's counsel. A small man in the third row sprang up and attempted to flee the courtroom, but he was collared by an attendant and admitted he had heard of apples in a lute. He was arrested and placed in the judge's lap. The prosecution then asked for a stay, as did also the defense, and the court ordered a pair of stays. The next morning the prosecution asked the prisoner that the case be dropped, as the judge had hung himself to a bridge-lamp with the stays. The true story then came out, the Riff revealing himself as a scenario writer anxious for romance.

"Fox was gnawing on my vitals," he blubbered. The words had hardly left his mouth when Flight-Commander Noah Beery and Wing-Lieutenant Gary Cooper burst in with the news that they had consulted the scared chickens on the Sibylline Hill; a dark man was about to cross their path. Caps were thrown in the air, you may be sure, for the boys at St. Witmark's had been expecting the mail-man for several days. Could that be his step in the corridor now? Everybody waited with beating hearts, each licking his lips in anticipation of smoking plum puddings and tasty sliced surgeon blemished with whipped cream. Suddenly the silver snarl of a bugle rang out into the clearing house at the head of their debit columns, brandishing felt pen-wipers. In a trice the red varmints had vamoosed in terror on their pintos. A cry of exultation met the gallant deliverers of the fort, for the tedium had almost given out and now there was fresh tedium for all. And that, fellow-members of the board of directors of the Whitebait Pay Bathroom Company, that, I say, is the meaning behind our motto, "If it's a Whitebait, you can take your dinner guests in evening clothes to look at it." Thank you.

WHAT'S YOUR NITRATE (NIGHT RATE, GET IT?) CHIRRUPED THE CHEMIST

Don't pluck everything you see in the Basque country, boys. You have to watch out for those poisonous berets. **Voice Over the Phone**—*"Is this the Weather Bureau? Will we have a shower tonight, mister?"* **Fiendish Fred, the Weather Tycoon**—*"For Heaven's sake, don't bother me! If you need one, take it and send me a bill!"*

OH MR. PERELMAN ARENT YOU THE CRAZIEST THING! CACKLED THE CUTIE

Put on your clean shirt, Benny, we're going to take out a couple of female acrobats. "Hey, information given out here?" shouted an excited visitor in a museum. "Yes, sir, it has," was the languid comment of the attendant. Thank God, here comes the United States cavalry from Fort Dodge!